Christmas

P9-DOB-978

MOUNT PLEASANT

Discard

Discard

Christmas Cookies

Christmas Cookies

50 RECIPES TO TREASURE FOR THE HOLIDAY SEASON

Lisa Zwirn

PHOTOGRAPHS BY CORINNE PLANCHE

WM

WILLIAM MORROW
An Imprint of HarperCollins*Publishers*

OCT 27 2008 MTP
641.8654
Z98c

Dedication

To my mother, Michele, who showed me how to cook

To my late father, Bernard, who taught me how to write
(and, perchance, to dream)

And to my husband, Mark, and sons, Alex and Todd,
who love to eat . . . especially cookies.

CHRISTMAS COOKIES. Copyright © 2008 by Lisa B. Zwirn. Photographs copyright © by Corinne Planche. All rights reserved. Printed in South China. No part of this book may be used or reproduced in any manner whatsoever without written permission except in the case of brief quotations embodied in critical articles and reviews. For information address HarperCollins Publishers, 10 East 53rd Street, New York, NY 10022.

HarperCollins books may be purchased for educational, business, or sales promotional use. For information please write: Special Markets Department, HarperCollins Publishers, 10 East 53rd Street, New York, NY 10022.

FIRST EDITION

Designed by Vertigo Design NYC

LIBRARY OF CONGRESS CATALOGING-IN-PUBLICATION DATA

Zwirn, Lisa B.

Christmas cookies: 50 recipes to treasure for the holiday season / Lisa B. Zwirn; photographs by Corinne Planche.—1st ed.

p. cm.

Includes index.

ISBN 978-0-06-137696-2

1. Cookies. 2. Christmas cookery. I. Title.

TX772.Z95 2008

641.8'654—dc22

2007031176

08 09 10 11 12 ID3/SCP 10 9 8 7 6 5 4 3 2 1

Contents

Acknowledgments

This book was a joy to write—really, what could be more fun than baking batches of yummy cookies and eating them with friends and family?—but what made it particularly special was sharing the experience with Corinne Planche, friend and neighbor, whose beautiful photographs grace these pages. From the get-go, Corinne was as excited as I was about the project, and her creativity and skill turned mere cookies into the most spectacular holiday treats.

To our favorite cookie monsters, Alex, Todd, Pierre-Edouard, Valerian, and Eugenie, who eagerly devoured and honestly critiqued the platefuls upon platefuls of treats set before them. To Mark and Patrick, too, may your waistlines never suffer from too many cookies.

To Carla Glasser, my agent, who on faith and trust gave me this fantastic opportunity, I am very grateful. To my cousin Patricia Shimm—thank you, thank you!—for putting the bug in Carla's ear. To David Sweeney, director of cookbooks at William Morrow, and Stephanie Fraser, my editor, who were so helpful and enjoyable to work with; it was smooth sailing from the moment we were introduced.

My brother, Richard Zwirn, offered oodles of suggestions and for that, as well as for his genuine interest and enthusiasm, I'm truly appreciative. Thank you to the women who tested some of the recipes: my mom and cookie-loving friends Andrea Pyenson, Catherine Walthers, and Bridie Hilperts.

And, finally, a big thank-you to my husband, Mark Granoff, whose keen sense of taste can discern a great cookie from a second-rate treat and for providing unflagging support through many months of floury surfaces, a kitchen sink perpetually filled with mixing bowls, and unavoidable overeating. Never did he seem to mind logging a few extra miles on his bike to burn off those excess cookie calories.

Introduction

Christmas is a holiday that holds different meanings for different people, but I'd venture to say that baking and eating sweet things is universal. Some cultures celebrate with traditional cakes, pies, and breads, but I'd have to say again that none of these is as widely understood and loved as Christmas cookies. At some point, probably centuries ago, the words *Christmas* and *cookies* became inextricably linked and now their various flavors, shapes, and colors bring joy to holiday revelers and bakers everywhere. Despite their simplicity—that is, compared with other, more complicated desserts—cookies have become a symbol of holiday cheer, enjoyed by young and old, baked by novice and expert, and used as a currency of love and caring.

What, then, you might ask, makes a cookie a Christmas cookie? The simple answer is that these treats are traditionally baked and served—and reserved—for the holiday season. The recipes might reflect age-old family or cultural traditions or might be more recent favorites that have become part of the annual festivities. In either case, the bite-size treats have a way of shaping memories and helping to preserve the magic of the season.

The other reasons why specific cookies are featured at Christmastime are more mundane. For one, their flavors belong to winter. Traditional spices such as cinnamon, nutmeg, ginger, and clove and sweeteners such as molasses, honey, and maple syrup make the treats rich-tasting and wonderfully fragrant. Flavors of peppermint and eggnog delight with their once-a-year appearances. Of course, an even more obvious giveaway to those treats destined for the holiday table or festive gift boxes is their familiar shapes and colors. From stars and bells to snowmen and Christmas trees, decorated with red and green sugar crystals, colorful icings, or wintry dustings of powdered sugar, these are cookies dressed in their finest holiday splendor.

What's most important, however, is that all the sweet, buttery, spicy, colorful goodness tastes spectacular. Only the best and freshest ingredients should go into making Christmas cookies. Pull out all the stops and buy the finest chocolate, good-quality butter, and fresh supplies of nuts and dried fruits. Bring out the enchanting aromas of the season by updating your spice rack. Replenish your supplies of flour, sugar, and leaveners. And last, but by no means least, make sure all your equipment is in good working order, your cookie sheets and baking pans clean, and all the necessary utensils and holiday cookie cutters handy. Oh, and stock up on parchment paper. It's a pan washer's best friend.

For the holiday baker, the baking ritual is as much a part of the season's preparation as decorating the house and hitting the shopping malls. Over the years I've discovered that Christmas cookie bakers usually fall into one of two categories. The early birds head to the kitchen in October, getting a jump start on the season by piling layers upon layers of cookies in their freezers. These folks subscribe to the useful maxim of "don't put off till tomorrow what you can get done today" and are well stocked months ahead. The other school can best be described as "wait to bake," and its members believe that only in December does holiday baking feel right. This group spends full days and even longer nights in the kitchen, churning out scads of cookies just before a Christmas party or gift-giving occasion.

But no matter what month it is, the holiday cookie baker jumps fearlessly into the kitchen, surrounded by her or his *batterie de cuisine* and grocery bags loaded with ingredients, primed to scoop flour, beat butter, melt chocolate, and whisk icing. What everyone realizes (usually at some ungodly hour and dozens of cookies later) is that the bounty is best shared. Perhaps this is how the tradition of gifting Christmas cookies began: as the result of overeager production! Yet what could be more heartfelt than to wrap up tins of homemade cookies and shower them upon friends and family? We might also contribute the treats to cookie swaps, bake sales, office parties, and our children's classrooms. Of course, we'll make sure to leave plenty in cookie jars for our family and lucky neighbors to enjoy. Nobody doesn't like Christmas cookies.

Whether you're just starting the tradition of holiday baking or have been doing it for years, all cooks need at least a handful of reliably good recipes that are sure to please. Unearthing new recipes also satisfies an inherent curiosity that I believe all bakers share. My goal in writing this book was to provide cookie bakers everywhere, including the early birds, last-minute bakers, experienced cooks, and novices, with recipes for traditional treats as well as for a few surprises that might soon become favorites.

Don't let the small size of this book fool you. Consider it the best of the best. I baked hundreds of different cookies to come up with these fabulous fifty that include something for everyone: treats for chocoholics, holiday shapes for children (which can be baked and decorated by the little ones, too), luxurious sandwich cookies, and plenty of spiced rounds, buttery wafers, and decadent bars. It's a collection you'll never tire of. In fact, I hope you won't confine yourself to baking these treasures only in the few months—or weeks—leading up to Christmas. Many are as wonderful in May as they are in December.

So let's start baking. It's the surest way I know to get into the holiday spirit. Whip up a batch of Chocolate Crinkles, Viennese Crescents, Toffee Bars, or Ginger Coins—or any other cookie in this book—and watch your mood soar and smiles come to the faces of those who happily nibble on your creations.

CHAPTER ONE

The Basics of Cookie Making

A GREAT COOKIE IS MADE FROM FRESH, QUALITY INGREDIENTS. IF YOU THINK OF THE LITTLE ROUNDS AND BARS AS JUST COMPACT CARRIERS OF FLAVOR, YOU'LL SEE HOW IMPORTANT EVERY STICK OF BUTTER, OUNCE OF CHOCOLATE, TEASPOON OF SPICE, AND CUP OF NUTS IS TO THE END RESULT. WHAT YOU MIX IN IS WHAT YOU'LL TASTE, SO KEEP THE PHRASE "QUALITY IN, QUALITY OUT" FOREMOST IN YOUR MIND AS YOU SHOP FOR INGREDIENTS.

Making cookies also requires a heaping spoonful of patience. Chocolate must be melted slowly so it doesn't burn, butter and sugar must be beaten sufficiently until creamy, and, in many recipes, the dough must be chilled to provide the best rolling and baking results. It's important not to take shortcuts or else the taste and texture of the cookies will suffer. If you're in a hurry, check out the Quick and Easy list on page 131.

There are two shortcuts, however, that you're free to take. Both of these, in a small but significant way, forever changed my cookie-baking routine for the better, allowing me to be more spontaneous and efficient.

1 BUTTER MUST BE SOFT AND PLIABLE TO BE PROPERLY CREAMED, but how often do we forget to take the sticks out of the refrigerator ahead of time? If you're very careful, butter can be softened in the microwave without affecting its usability. Here's how: Place one stick, still in its paper wrapping (or unwrap it and place it on a microwave-safe plate or a sheet of wax paper), in the microwave. Turn the machine on high for ten or eleven seconds. No more! You don't want to melt the butter, which would change the consistency of the dough and the cookies. When you lightly squeeze a stick of softened butter it should leave impressions of your fingers, but it shouldn't feel mushy. With this little trick, there's no more waiting for butter to soften before you can bake.

2 TRY TO BE ONE STEP AHEAD OF YOUR OVEN. Have the next batch of cookies ready to go on a clean sheet of parchment paper. When a cookie sheet comes out of the oven, slide the parchment with the baked cookies onto a rack, and then slide the parchment with the formed dough onto the sheet and immediately place it in the oven. (Do this quickly because dough should never sit on a hot sheet for more than a few seconds.) Now there's no more waiting for hot cookie sheets to cool before they can be used again.

Otherwise, a cookie recipe, like all baking recipes, is a formula. Yes, that bowl full of yummy ingredients is bound up in the science of chemistry. So read through the recipe carefully, follow it precisely, and measure accurately; your cookie baking will not only be loads of fun but successful!

A QUICK WORD ON HOW THIS BOOK IS ORGANIZED: The recipes are grouped by the type of cookie, or more specifically, by how the cookie is made. Drop cookies are formed by dropping the dough onto a cookie sheet with a spoon. Rolled cookies are stamped into various shapes from dough that is rolled out. Bar cookies are baked in baking pans and cut into bars. And so on. A few treats at the end of the book don't even require an oven. The book is organized this way because it allows you to easily locate the recipes you feel most comfortable trying or have the appropriate equipment for. There are helpful tips for making each type of cookie in their respective chapters.

For those bakers, however, who care less about cookie type and more about what's inside—say, chocolate or lemon or no nuts—there's a listing of cookies by flavor at the back of the book on pages 130 to 131. Use this list for inspiration and to satisfy your cravings!

Cookie-Baking Guidelines

Here are the key steps and rules for successful cookie baking. Read them over a few times, then embed them in your cookie-baking routine.

- Before you start, make sure you have all the necessary ingredients and enough time for pre- and post-baking tasks. Many recipes require prep work, such as toasting nuts, grating citrus zest, and chopping chocolate, before you can actually start assembling the dough. Some doughs need to be chilled for an hour or more before baking. And a few bar cookies shouldn't be left to cool for too long after they come out of the oven; they must be cut while still warm or else they become too hard or crumbly to slice.

- Preheat the oven for at least fifteen minutes before baking.

- You'll achieve the most consistent results when you bake one cookie sheet at a time on a rack in the middle of the oven. If you want to use two sheets to move the job along (after first checking to make sure the recipe suggests it), place the racks in the upper and lower thirds of the oven with at least four inches between them so heat can circulate. Ideally, the bottom rack should be at the top of the lower third of the oven and the top rack at the bottom of the top third. When using two sheets, it's important to rotate them from top to bottom and front to back about halfway through baking to allow the cookies to bake evenly. Do it carefully, yet quickly, because the oven temperature will drop the longer the oven door is open. If one sheet of cookies is done before the other, pull it from the oven.

- Follow the recipe instructions for shaping the cookies to the proper size or rolling the dough to the appropriate thickness in order to get uniform results and the indicated yield. Cookies of the recommended size will bake evenly in the time suggested.

- Don't crowd the cookie sheet. Leave the suggested amount of space around the cookies, which accounts for spreading and allows the oven heat to circulate and brown the cookies properly.

- ALWAYS check the cookies a minute or two before the suggested minimum baking time. Your oven may run hot or your cookies may be smaller or thinner than the size suggested, causing them to bake faster. That being said, if your cookies take a few minutes longer, that's okay, too. Ovens vary tremendously. Follow the visual clues for doneness provided in each recipe. Also, remember that most cookies firm up as they cool, so resist the temptation to add minutes to the baking time to produce crispier treats. It will usually just result in dry, overbaked, and possibly burnt-tasting cookies.

- When the cookies are done, immediately remove the cookie sheet from the oven. Unless a recipe directs otherwise, remove the cookies from the sheet one at a time, using a thin metal spatula, and place them on a cooling rack. For particularly fragile cookies, it's best to slide the parchment paper (with the cookies on it) onto a rack and let the cookies sit until firm enough to place directly on the rack to finish cooling.

- Always let cookie sheets cool before putting on the next batch of dough. Dough on a hot sheet will start to melt and spread, changing the shape, texture, and even the taste of the baked cookie. To speed things up, however, you can follow the shortcut on page 1 and have the next batch ready to go on a clean sheet of parchment. Slide the parchment onto the hot cookie sheet and immediately place the sheet in the oven. (The key is to not let the dough sit on a hot baking sheet before it goes into the oven.)

Chilling and Freezing Cookie Dough

Refrigerating cookie dough allows it to rest and firm up before it is rolled and shaped. In some recipes, such as the Chocolate Crinkles and all the Slice and Bake cookies, the dough is impossible to work with until it has had a good, long chill. In general, whenever dough needs to be chilled before baking, it can be refrigerated for longer than the time specified, usually up to three or four days. The dough will harden, but it will soften again to rolling or shaping consistency after sitting at room temperature for about an hour.

Cookie doughs with high butter content freeze well, usually for up to three to four months. The type of cookie will dictate whether the dough should be frozen in a disk shape (if it's to be rolled out), a ball (for drop or hand-shaped cookies), or a log (for slicing). In all cases, make sure to wrap it snugly in plastic wrap and, for extra protection against frost, secure it with a layer of foil or in a heavy-duty plastic bag. Label and date the package because frozen blobs and logs are difficult to identify after a few months. You might even want to attach a piece of paper with the baking instructions so you don't have to hunt for the recipe when it's time to bake. Thaw frozen dough in the fridge overnight or, if needed sooner, for an hour or two at room temperature.

Storing Cookies

Step number one of proper cookie storage is to cool the cookies completely. Treats that are still warm from the oven create a steamy environment, perfect for turning their textures soft and mushy.

Step two is to choose containers with tight-fitting lids, be they plastic, metal, or ceramic; or you could use sealable plastic bags. If wrapping cookies in foil, first surround them in a layer of plastic wrap or wax paper for a more secure package because foil is easily punctured. Iced, glazed, or sticky cookies, as well as those that are particularly fragile, should be stored in layers separated by sheets of wax or parchment paper.

And the final, cardinal rule of cookie storage is that one container doesn't fit all. For your cookies to taste as good as when they were first baked, separate the different flavors and textures. Mild-flavored buttery rounds will acquire notes of spice or citrus if packed next to cookies with these stronger flavors. And never should a crunchy meet a softy! Crisp cookies will lose their delectable crunch if stored alongside moist or chewy treats.

Every recipe in this book includes storage recommendations. Unless speci-fied otherwise, cookies should be stored in airtight containers at room tempera-ture. A time frame for how long the cookies can be kept before their flavor and texture become less than perfect is also included. While many cookies taste their absolute best on the day they're baked or as close to it as possible, others, such as spice cookies, develop their flavorful nuances over a few days' time. These treats, as well as super buttery varieties like sablés, sugar cookies, and shortbread, can be kept for weeks. Iced and filled cookies generally don't last as long, nor do they freeze well. (An exception is the Fig Half-Moons.) If you want to freeze cookies that will be iced or glazed, freeze them undecorated. Thaw the cookies at room temperature on wire racks for a few hours, then decorate them as you would if they were fresh.

Freezing Cookies

To freeze those cookies that freeze well (and not all cookies do, so check the specific recipe), secure them with a snug double wrapping to protect them from freezer burn. Wrap the cookies first in plastic, then enclose them in a layer of foil or tuck them inside a heavy-duty freezer bag. When stacking the treats, use wax or parchment paper to separate the layers.

Frozen cookies can be thawed in the refrigerator or at room temperature. If thawing at room temperature, open the package slightly so moisture isn't trapped inside. Some varieties, such as the Fig Half-Moons, Cornmeal Currant Cookies, and biscotti, benefit from a few minutes heating and recrisping in a 350°F or 375°F oven. (And then again, some of us love eating frozen cookies!)

CHAPTER TWO

Giving Cookies

HOMEMADE COOKIES MAKE GREAT GIFTS. NOT ONLY ARE THEY DELICIOUS, BUT THE TREATS ARE AN OFFERING OF YOUR TIME AND LOVE. FOR CHRISTMAS, THE SKY'S THE LIMIT AS TO THE NUMBER OF WAYS YOU CAN PACKAGE THEM: PLACE THE TREATS ON A DECORATIVE PLATE, WRAP THEM UP IN AN ATTRACTIVE TIN, BOX, OR BASKET, OR PILE THEM INTO A SMALL HOLIDAY-THEMED SHOPPING BAG. COLORED PLASTIC WRAP OR CELLOPHANE, DECORATIVE TISSUE AND WRAPPING PAPER, AND PLENTY OF RIBBONS AND BOWS WILL MAKE THE PACKAGING FESTIVE.

Always attach cards or labels with the cookie names written on them along with a list of ingredients in case of possible allergies. Even better, include the recipes.

When packaging cookies to give (in person) or send, follow the same rules for storing them: Keep flavors and textures separated so they taste and crunch as intended. Enclose same-kind cookies in plastic wrap or small, sealable plastic bags. Iced or glazed treats should be separated by layers of wax paper so they don't stick together.

The best cookies to mail are those that are sturdy and keep well. These include shortbread and other firm buttery cookies, and most bar, sugar, and spice cookies, which will stay fresh for a week or more. Meringues, sandwich and filled cookies, and any other fragile treats are best enjoyed closer to home.

When mailing cookies, pack them in a holiday tin, paper box, or plastic container. (A clean shoe box works, too.) Pack the treats close together, cushioned with bubble wrap or tissue paper for extra protection, and make sure there's no room for wiggling. Think snug. And go for holiday color. Buy some colored cellophane, plastic wrap, or tissue paper to line the inside of the container. Peeling away the layers to see what's inside is part of the excitement.

Linzer Cookies (page 99)

The container(s) should then be packed in a slightly larger box for mailing. Create a tight fit inside the carton by using crumpled newspaper or foam packing peanuts to keep the cookie container(s) from bouncing around. How you send the package may depend on your holiday budget, but shipping by pony express won't help your cookies. It's best to ship overnight or by priority mail, which typically takes two days, to guarantee that the treats arrive in tasty condition.

GOOD COOKIES FOR MAILING

Chocolate Espresso Wafers	65	Peanut Brittle Bars	113
Chocolate Shortbread Wedges	115	Pecan Sandies	67
Cornmeal Currant Cookies	43	Pinwheel Cookies	63
Cranberry Pistachio Biscotti	74	Rocky Road Bites	126
Dutch Spice Cookies	44	Rum Balls	129
Ginger Coins	59	Sugar Cookies	46
Hazelnut Biscotti	72	Toffee Bars	120
Mexican Chocolate Snowballs	40	Turtle Bars	122

One More Gift Idea

Give dough. Cookie dough, that is. The recipient then has the opportunity to bake cookies whenever the mood strikes. Load the dough into sturdy plastic tubs (unless it's rolled into a log for Slice and Bake cookies) and attach baking instructions. Check out the list of Make-Ahead and Freeze Cookie Dough on page 131 for yummy options. Date the package and instruct that the dough should be frozen if not used within two days.

CHAPTER THREE

Holiday Cookie Parties

FOR COOKS WHO ARE ALWAYS LOOKING OVER THEIR SHOULDER AT WHAT THEIR NEIGHBORS OR FRIENDS ARE BAKING, A COOKIE SWAP IS A GREAT OPPORTUNITY TO LEARN A FEW NEW TRICKS AND GATHER A BUNCH OF GREAT RECIPES. FOR THE NOVICE, IT'S AN OPPORTUNITY TO START BUILDING A COOKIE REPERTOIRE. AND FOR THE COOKIE MONSTER IN ALL OF US, IT'S SIMPLY DELICIOUS!

How to Host a Holiday Cookie Swap

Here's how a cookie swap (or exchange) typically works: you bring the required amount of cookies, say, two or three dozen, and enough copies of your recipe for all the attendees, and in exchange you get to assemble a container full of everyone else's treats to take home. Won't your family be thrilled when you leave with a tin of the familiar and return with an assortment they've never seen before!

Hosting a holiday cookie swap is easy. First, pick a date a few weeks before Christmas. Second, send out invitations requesting that guests bring a specified amount of their chosen cookie (usually enough for each attendee to get at least three or four of each kind) along with enough copies of the typed or handwritten recipe. Also, ask your guests to bring a plate or container for carrying their goodies home. (Occasionally, the host will graciously provide this.) As the host, you'll need to supply plastic wrap, foil, and small plastic bags for wrapping up the treats. Offer an assortment of beverages, such as eggnog, mulled cider, wine, coffee, or tea, to quench cookie-logged thirsts.

As the guests arrive, display their offerings on holiday-decorated tables and countertops. Give everyone time to stroll around and study the treats. After the oohs and aahs, it's nice to have the bakers share a little history or anecdotes about their recipes. Then comes the fun part: attendees grab a container and help themselves to the allotted amount of cookies. Tasting should be wholeheartedly encouraged! The folks back home don't have to know how many cookies you started with.

How to Host a Cookie-Making or Cookie-Decorating Party

These two party ideas are designed mostly for kids, but they're certainly not exclusive to children. Maybe the man or woman in your life has hidden cookie-decorating talent. For the inner baker in most of us, but especially the little ones, it's great fun plunging wrist-deep into cookie dough, rolling it out, and stamping gingerbread people, sugar cookie Christmas trees, and stained-glass stars. What joy shaking out red and green sugar crystals over holiday shapes awaiting their turn for the oven! Expect plenty of smiles and mess. (Warning: Neatniks should let others host these events.) Everyone gets to eat her or his creations or take them home.

For a **COOKIE-MAKING PARTY**, the host can provide the ingredients, equipment, and utensils, or the guests can chip in. Make sure to have plenty of mixing bowls, cookie sheets, cookie cutters in holiday shapes, rolls of parchment paper, and pot holders. Activities are best organized into stations, such as the beating and mixing station, dough-shaping area, and rolling and cookie-cutting surface. Everyone, however, gets to work the nibbling station!

For doughs that need to be refrigerated before being shaped or rolled, each one can be chilled while another variety is assembled and/or baked. The host can start the party off by preparing one or two doughs ahead, which can be ready to roll after the bakers assemble their first batch. Bar cookies, macaroons, and most drop cookies can go right into the oven after they're prepared.

Sugar Cookies (page 46)

For a cookie-making party, try these fun-to-make cookies:

For a **COOKIE-DECORATING PARTY**, the host usually provides plain sugar cookies and/or gingerbread shapes and plenty of decorations. The host can bake all the cookies ahead of time or, better yet, send out a recipe a week before the party and ask volunteers to each bake a few dozen. If you're pressed for time, you could even arrange to purchase plain cutouts from a local bakery.

At this event, the fun is in the decorating, so you'll want to have a generous supply of sugars, candies, and icing as well as the necessary tools. Icing is decorative on its own and serves as the glue that allows the other decorations to stick to the cookie. You'll find a recipe for Royal Icing and a simpler Confectioners' Sugar Icing on pages 48 and 56, respectively.

Sugar Cookies with Stained Glass (page 49)

For a cookie-decorating party, you'll need the following items:

EDIBLES

Confectioners' sugar

Decorative sugars, including colored
sugars and coarse sugars, such as
sanding, pearl, and sparkling

Egg-white powder (also called
meringue powder)

Food colorings

Homemade or store-bought icing

Mini candies (such as Red Hots and
mini M&Ms)

Multicolored nonpareils

Raisins and currants

Sliced almonds

Sprinkles (chocolate and multicolored)

Sweetened shredded coconut

TOOLS

Bowls (lots of small bowls or ramekins)

Frosting spreaders

Mini paintbrushes

Pastry brushes

Squeeze bottles, small plastic bags, and/
or pastry bags with different tips

Wax paper, plastic wrap, and foil

Sugar Cookies
(page 46)

CHAPTER FOUR

Key Ingredients for the Cookie Baker

TO REITERATE WHAT I SAID ON THE VERY FIRST PAGE, THE PHRASE "QUALITY IN, QUALITY OUT" SHOULD BE THE COOKIE BAKER'S MANTRA. WHEN IT COMES TO INGREDIENTS, USE THE BEST YOU CAN FIND OR AFFORD AND MAKE SURE EVERYTHING IS FRESH.

BAKING POWDER AND BAKING SODA: In cookies, these leavening agents help lift and lighten the texture of the dough. Baking soda also helps with browning. Although both tend to last a long time, baking powder, in particular, won't leaven if it's too old. Date the containers when you purchase them and throw them out after a year.

BUTTER: Nothing's better than real butter, especially in cookies, in which its flavor is so discernible. Use only unsalted butter, which contains less water and is generally fresher-tasting than salted butter. The first step of most cookie recipes is beating the butter, and to do this it must be soft but not mushy. Squeezing a stick with your fingers should just leave their impressions. Check out the shortcut on page 1 for when the butter is cold but you're in the mood to bake!

When adding butter to dry ingredients in a food processor, always cut it into one-tablespoon or smaller pieces so it can be absorbed evenly and with minimal processing.

Tip: Watch out for incorrectly aligned paper wrappers on sticks of butter when you're slicing off just a few tablespoons. Remove the wrapper, place it back over the butter with the measurement markings lined up properly, and slice off the amount you need.

CHOCOLATE: Good-quality chocolate makes a difference. What they say about wine—if you wouldn't want to drink it, don't cook with it—applies to chocolate: if you wouldn't want to eat it, don't bake with it.

When a recipe calls for bittersweet chocolate, choose one with at least 60 percent chocolate liquor, which is the combination of cocoa solids and cocoa butter or essentially everything that is derived from the cacao bean. Semisweet chocolate usually contains between 35 percent and 55 percent chocolate liquor. The rest of what's in chocolate is mostly sugar, so the higher the cocoa percentage, the more intense the chocolate flavor and the less sugar there is. Milk chocolate is sweeter than semisweet chocolate and has milk added. Unsweetened chocolate contains no sugar and is approximately 99 percent chocolate liquor.

To find a few brands you like, taste them out of the wrapper and in baked goods. Before baking with any chocolate, make sure it's fresh; the chocolate should be glossy and firm. Store all chocolate in a cool, dark, and dry place.

TWO PIECES OF ADVICE: (1) Don't use semisweet chocolate chips (morsels) for any of the chocolate called for in this book. (The only exception might be for the kid-friendly Peanut Butter Chocolate Squares if you'd rather not waste your good dark chocolate.) The chips are sweeter and less chocolaty than regular block chocolate and they don't melt as well. (2) If you buy chocolate in large chunks that your market has chopped, wrapped, and labeled, taste it before you bake with it. I once purchased a one-pound slab marked "62 percent bittersweet chocolate" only to discover—thankfully, before I baked with it!—that it was unsweetened chocolate.

MELTING CHOCOLATE: The key to melting chocolate is to do it gently so it doesn't burn or turn grainy. It's best to use the double-boiler method by either using a set of nesting saucepans (called a double boiler) or setting a stainless steel or glass bowl over the rim of a saucepan containing about an inch or two of barely simmering water. The bottom of the bowl should not touch the water. Always start with chocolate that has been chopped into small chunks and stir often. Remove the bowl from the heat before the chocolate is fully melted and stir to melt the remaining pieces. Be careful not to let the chocolate come in contact with water (or steam) as just a few drops of liquid can cause it to "seize" and become a grainy mess.

Chocolate can also be melted in the microwave. Place chopped chocolate in a microwave-safe bowl or glass measuring cup and melt it in twenty- to thirty-second increments on medium power, stirring after each interval. Stirring is important because the chocolate will continue to maintain its shape even when it's melted.

COCOA POWDER: For baking, use only unsweetened cocoa powder, which comes two ways: natural and Dutch-processed. The latter has been treated with an alkali to neutralize the acidity in chocolate, leaving it with a slightly less intense flavor and darker color. When natural (nonalkalized) cocoa is used, the recipe usually contains baking soda, which helps tame the acidity. If the recipe doesn't specify which kind to use, natural cocoa is fine.

COCONUT: For the two recipes in this book that call for coconut, use the sweetened shredded variety that is readily available in supermarkets.

DAIRY PRODUCTS: "Heavy cream" and "whipping cream" can be used interchangeably in these recipes. (The difference is typically a tiny bit more butterfat in heavy cream.) For recipes calling for milk, 1 percent or 2 percent milk can replace whole milk. Regular cream cheese is preferable to low-fat versions; don't use whipped cream cheese or nonfat products because the cookies' taste and texture will be affected.

DRIED FRUIT: Dried fruits are, of course, dried, but they should be fresh. Purchase soft, moist, flavorful fruit, and discard any that's been hanging around too long, especially if the fruit is rock hard or (yikes!) moldy.

EGGS: Use USDA-grade large eggs and always store them in their original carton in the refrigerator. When a recipe calls for just yolks or whites, reserve the other in a small cup or ramekin, covered with plastic wrap, in the refrigerator for up to a few days. When separating the whites from the yolks, make sure not a drop of yolk (or any other fat) ends up in the whites or they won't beat properly.

Tip: When life gives you egg whites, make macaroons or meringues. When egg yolks pile up, bake Pecan Sandies, Orange Poppy Seed Drops, Eggnog Cookies, Toasted Coconut Sablés, or Walnut Stars.

EGG-WHITE POWDER (MERINGUE POWDER): For health reasons, it's safer to use dried egg whites than raw whites in a recipe in which they won't be heated, such as Royal Icing.

EXTRACTS AND FLAVORINGS: For the tastiest cookies, use pure extracts rather than imitation or artificial flavorings. For flavored oils such as peppermint, hazelnut, and lemon, remember that a little goes a long way.

FLOUR: The cookies in this book were tested with all-purpose flour. I used King Arthur unbleached all-purpose flour, but bleached flour is fine, too. Just make sure the flour isn't too old.

To measure flour, lightly spoon it into a flat-rimmed measuring cup meant for dry ingredients (see page 24) and sweep off the excess with the straight edge of a knife or bench scraper. Don't shake the cup to settle the flour or pack it in, as this will increase the amount of flour in the cup.

FOOD COLORING: The liquid food colorings available at most supermarkets are fine, but natural dyes or professional pastes and powders may be preferable if you're planning to tint large amounts of icing.

NUTS: Nuts are a favorite ingredient in Christmas cookies all over the world, so you'll find many varieties of nutty treats—made with almonds, hazelnuts, peanuts, pecans, pistachios, and walnuts—in this book. If you or anyone you're baking for is allergic, consult the Cookies Without Nuts list on page 131 for safe options.

Before you bake, smell and taste the nuts to make sure they're fresh. If you buy in bulk or only use them sporadically, store them in the freezer for up to one year. When nuts are left too long at room temperature, the oil in them turns rancid, giving them a terrible funky-oily smell and taste.

Most cookie recipes call for nuts to be chopped or ground. The various sizes called for can be somewhat confusing, so here's a quick summary: coarsely chopped (a large nut cut into 2 to 3 pieces); chopped or medium-chopped (about ¼-inch pieces); finely chopped (about ⅛- to ³⁄₁₆-inch bits); ground or finely ground (like grainy sand); and nut meal/flour (a slightly gritty powder).

TOASTING NUTS: Toasting nuts brings out their flavor and crunch. In recipes in which the nuts will be chopped or ground, they're usually toasted (and cooled) prior to chopping. Occasionally, as in the Toffee Bars, I like to toast chopped nuts so all cut sides turn golden.

To toast nuts, spread the amount you need in a single layer on a baking sheet and place in a 325°F oven. (You can also toast nuts at 350°F, but watch them carefully and give them a little less time.) Stir the nuts or shake the pan once or twice during toasting. Chopped, sliced, or slivered nuts or small varieties such as pine nuts toast the fastest, in about 4 to 7 minutes. Walnuts, pecans, and pistachios will take between 8 and 12 minutes, and harder nuts such as whole almonds and hazelnuts may require up to 10 to 14 minutes. Let your nose be your guide. When you smell their delicious aroma and they appear lightly golden, they're done. Take care not to burn them. You can use a toaster oven, but watch carefully because they generally toast faster in the smaller space.

Hazelnuts (also called filberts) require the additional step of removing their papery skins. While the nuts are still warm, place them in a dish towel and rub them with the towel to loosen and remove the skins. Don't worry if some of it refuses to come off; totally bare nuts aren't necessary for any of these recipes.

SALT: Don't be surprised to find salt in most of the recipes in this book. Salt is a flavor enhancer, as much in sweets as in savory cooking. Use regular table salt, not coarse salt.

SPICES: Spices should smell and taste like they're supposed to. If the jar of ground cinnamon or ginger has been hanging around for longer than a year, it's probably stale. It's best to buy whole nutmeg and grate it just before using. Ditto for allspice and cloves. Use a Microplane or other fine-holed grater for nutmeg and a spice (or coffee) grinder for allspice berries and cloves.

SUGAR AND OTHER SWEETENERS: Stock your pantry with granulated, confectioners' (also called powdered, icing, or 10X), and light and dark brown sugars. Superfine sugar is sometimes used for ultradelicate cookies and meringues.

For decorating, it's nice to have an assortment of colored, sparkling, and pearl sugars. Sweeteners like maple syrup, molasses, and honey add flavor and moisture and, along with corn syrup, give cookies a slightly softer, chewy texture.

Note that when a recipe calls for just "sugar" it is always granulated sugar; otherwise a different type of sugar will be specified.

ZEST: When you grate the peel or rind of a citrus fruit, gather only the colored part, not the bitter white pith below it. To measure finely grated zest, lightly pack it in a measuring spoon.

Orange Poppy
Seed Drops
(page 76)

CHAPTER FIVE

Key Tools for the Cookie Baker

AT FIRST GLANCE, THIS MAY APPEAR LIKE A LENGTHY LIST OF TOOLS AND EQUIPMENT YOU SHOULD HAVE, BUT CHANCES ARE YOU ALREADY OWN MOST OF THE ITEMS. AND WHILE SOME ARE TRULY NECESSARY FOR SUCCESSFUL COOKIE BAKING, OTHERS ARE JUST USEFUL OR TIME-SAVING. THERE'S ONLY ONE THING YOU SHOULDN'T SKIMP ON AND THAT'S QUALITY COOKIE SHEETS.

BAKING PANS AND SHEETS: Choose shiny, light-colored (dark metal causes excess browning), heavy-gauge aluminum (or aluminized steel) baking pans in the following sizes: 8-inch square, 9-inch square, 9 × 13 × 2-inch rectangle, and 10½ × 15½ × 1-inch jelly roll pan. Baking sheets come in all different sizes and have four short sides, about ½ to 1 inch high, to prevent foods from sliding off. These are useful for toasting nuts and baking some cookies such as biscotti. Otherwise, cookies should be baked on cookie sheets. (See below.)

BENCH SCRAPER: This tool, also called a pastry or dough scraper, is a small, rectangular piece of steel with a thick handle along the top. It's practical for scraping or lifting dough off a work surface and perfect for cutting bar cookies. I found one with an added benefit: it's marked in inches along the bottom and up one side to facilitate measuring the thickness and/or diameter of dough and unbaked cookies.

BOWLS: Cookie bakers need lots of bowls in various sizes. Stainless steel is best for most uses; choose those that are deeper rather than shallow and wide in order to prevent ingredients from flying out during beating. Also have a few glass bowls for microwave heating.

COOKIE CUTTERS: Holiday cookie bakers should have cutters in all kinds of holiday shapes as well as stars, hearts, diamonds, and scalloped (or fluted) rounds of different sizes. Cleaning and drying them well before storing will help preserve them. Dip cutters in flour before stamping if the dough sticks to them.

COOKIE SHEETS: Don't be tempted to buy thin, flimsy cookie sheets just because they cost less. You'll find that slightly more expensive, commercial-quality sheets will be worth their weight in perfectly baked cookies. Cookie sheets should be shiny, light-colored, heavy-gauge aluminum (or aluminized steel) pans that are hefty for their size so they won't buckle or warp over time. The standard size of approximately 13 × 15 inches fits in most ovens and allows heat to circulate all around it. Depending on the type of cookie, 9 to 12 (or up to 16 if they don't spread) will fit per sheet. Cookie sheets have one or two slightly raised or lipped sides that make it easy to grip the pan, while the rimless sides allow you to slide cookies, and parchment paper loaded with cookies, off and on. Don't use insulated or air-cushioned sheets, because they bake more slowly and prevent cookies from browning properly.

COOLING RACKS: Have at least two or three large wire racks to put cookies on to cool after they come out of the oven. Choose those with a small, square grid pattern and feet that raise the rack at least ¾ inch above a counter surface.

ELECTRIC MIXERS: Either a stand mixer or a handheld mixer will get the job done, and home bakers usually swear by one or the other. I use both, but I am particularly devoted to my good old hand mixer. I find it simpler and less cumbersome to use and I don't have to spend as much time scraping down the bowl. For batter or dough requiring a few minutes' beating or if the dough is particularly thick or heavy, a stand mixer with its paddle attachment will certainly give your arm a rest.

FOOD PROCESSOR: An indispensable tool in the baker's kitchen, a processor is perfect for grinding nuts, pureeing fruit sauces, combining dry and wet mixtures, and making vanilla sugar.

GRATER/ZESTER: A metal grater with small, sharp-edged holes is critical for grating fine zest from citrus fruits and for grating nutmeg. I think the classic Microplane grater produces the finest, most tender zest.

MEASURING CUPS AND SPOONS: Dry ingredients should be measured in sturdy, stainless-steel cups with straight rims. (Metal or hard plastic will hold its shape best and won't warp over the years.) The flat rim makes it easy to level off ingredients such as flour and sugar. Purchase one or two sets in the following sizes: 1 cup, ½ cup, ⅓ cup, and ¼ cup. Liquids should be measured in glass cups with spouts that are clearly marked in ¼-cup increments, ounces, and metric measurements. They should be heat resistant and microwave safe. Purchase 1-cup, 2-cup (1-pint), and 4-cup (1-quart) sizes. A mini 4-tablespoon (¼-cup) measure is perfect for small amounts of liquids such as milk and maple syrup. Have two sets of sturdy, stainless-steel measuring spoons in sizes from ⅛ teaspoon to 1 tablespoon.

PARCHMENT PAPER AND SILICONE BAKING MATS: Lining cookie sheets with parchment paper eliminates the need for greasing the sheets and saves you cleanup time. It also allows you to transfer a whole batch of baked cookies off a hot sheet and onto a rack to cool, and slide on a paper full of unbaked rounds. The paper can be reused for a few batches (just wipe off crumbs with a damp sponge) until either it gets too browned or stuck-on bits start to burn. Silicone mats are more expensive, but they are reusable for what might be years of baking. I favor parchment paper for its "sliding" benefits and because, in some cases, the mats hamper browning.

SCALE: Ingredients such as chocolate, nuts, dried fruits, and coconut are often specified in ounces rather than cup measures because one baker's chopped sizes or definition of "packed" or "heaping" may differ from another's. A reliable kitchen scale, either digital or spring-based, is therefore a necessity to accurately weigh these (and other) ingredients.

SPATULAS: You can never have too many spatulas. You'll need medium and large rubber (or silicone) spatulas for mixing, folding, and scraping dough from the sides of a bowl and the small, narrow kind for scraping foods from the inside of jars and measuring cups. Wide metal spatulas are essential for lifting cookies off cookie sheets and placing unbaked shapes on; and thin, narrow metal spatulas are useful for removing bar cookies from their pans. An offset spatula can be used for frosting bar cookies.

MISCELLANEOUS ITEMS

Saucepans of various sizes are a must for jobs such as melting butter, making caramel, and heating cream. A **kitchen timer** (or two) is essential for timing cookies in the oven. A **rolling pin** that's comfortable in your hands is necessary for producing rolled cookies. Keep a **ruler** or **metal measuring tape** handy for measuring the thickness, length, and width of rolled dough and the height of some cookies. You'll need a **wire whisk** for blending dry ingredients and beating eggs, a **pastry brush** for brushing egg wash on dough before baking, and mini **paintbrushes** for spreading icing on cookies. **Pastry bags** and **decorator tips** are used by professionals to pipe and decorate cookies, but to be honest they're not essential for any cookie in this book. If you like to use them, go ahead, but there are other, easier options for drizzling and piping icing, such as **squeeze bottles** (buy the ones with the smallest holes in the tops you can find) and **small plastic bags** (with a tiny hole snipped at one corner).

A **coffee grinder** is perfect for grinding whole spices such as cloves, allspice, and pepper. A few sharp **knives** are essential for chopping nuts, chocolate, and other ingredients, as well as for slicing logs of dough and cutting bar cookies. A **pizza wheel** (or pizza cutter) also works well for cutting bar cookies and shortbread. Other useful items are a **sifter** or a small **fine-mesh sieve** for dusting confectioners' sugar over cookies and sifting out the lumps in cocoa powder; a **cookie scoop** for portioning dough (these mini ice-cream scoops come in various sizes and are fun to use); and a **demitasse spoon** for teeny-weeny jobs such as filling wells in cookies with caramel or powdered candy. Last, but not least, you'll need **plastic wrap**, **aluminum foil**, **wax paper**, small (sandwich-size) and large (1-gallon) **sealable plastic bags**, and plenty of airtight **plastic containers** or **metal tins** for keeping all your goodies fresh!

Drop Cookies

Maple Walnut Cookies

MAKES ABOUT *32* COOKIES

Years ago—it was 1973, to be exact—my mother clipped cookbook author Jean Hewitt's recipe for Black Walnut Cakes from the *New York Times Magazine*. The cookies, which were frosted with maple icing, quickly became one of our winter favorites. I've made a few changes since then, including adding a little maple syrup to the dough, substituting butter for shortening, and toasting the walnuts to accentuate their flavor (any kind of walnuts will do). They're still a seasonal treat, perfect with a mug of hot chocolate.

1	cup walnuts
1¾	cups all-purpose flour
½	teaspoon baking soda
¼	teaspoon salt
8	tablespoons (1 stick) unsalted butter, softened
¾	cup packed light brown sugar
1	large egg
3	tablespoons pure maple syrup

MAPLE ICING

¼	cup pure maple syrup
2	tablespoons unsalted butter
1¼ to 1½ cups confectioners' sugar	

PREHEAT the oven to 350°F. Line 1 or 2 cookie sheets with parchment paper.

SPREAD the walnuts in a single layer on a small baking sheet. Toast in the oven for 6 to 8 minutes or just until you start to smell them. Transfer the nuts to a cutting board, and when cool enough to handle, chop coarse.

WHISK together the flour, baking soda, and salt in a small bowl.

USING an electric mixer, beat the butter in a large bowl until creamy. Add the brown sugar and beat until fully combined. Beat in the egg, then the maple syrup. With the beaters on low speed, mix in the flour mixture just until incorporated. Mix in the walnuts.

DROP the dough by slightly rounded tablespoonfuls onto the prepared sheet(s), arranging about 2 inches apart. Flatten the mounds with your fingers to about a ½-inch thickness. Bake for 13 to 15 minutes or until the cookies are golden and mostly firm to the touch. (If using 2 cookie sheets, rotate them from top to bottom and front to back about halfway through baking.) Transfer the cookies to a rack to cool completely.

FOR THE ICING: Place the maple syrup and butter in a small saucepan and heat, stirring, over low heat just until the butter melts. Remove from the heat and whisk in 1¼ cups of the confectioners' sugar, adding more as necessary to make a thick but spreadable icing. Using a frosting spreader or a table knife, glaze the tops of the cookies. Reheat the icing for a few seconds if it becomes too thick to spread. Let the cookies stand on a rack until the icing sets.

STORE, layered between sheets of wax paper, in an airtight container for up to 5 days.

Tips FOR MAKING DROP COOKIES

- Drop cookies are the easiest of the bunch. You just drop the dough by spoonfuls into mounds on the cookie sheet. For the first few "drops," use the recommended spoon size to get a feel for the correct amount. After that, just eyeball it. In some recipes the mounds are flattened to a certain height or diameter to make the cookies slightly thinner and more uniform. (This is particularly useful if they're going to be glazed.) Measure the first few with a ruler to know how thick or wide they should be.

- Actually, the word *drop* is a bit of a misnomer because in most cases the dough doesn't just drop from the spoon. It needs a little help. Use a finger of your free hand to push the dough off the spoon or use another spoon to do it.

- Drop-cookie dough is generally soft—too soft or sticky to roll out, for example—which causes it to spread during baking. The most extreme example of this is the Lace Cookie. Space the cookies as suggested in each recipe to give them room to grow.

- If you want to produce more uniformly round cookies, most drop doughs can be rolled into balls, but you'll need to chill the dough first to firm it up.

Brown Sugar Pecan Cookies

Whip up a batch of these cookies when guests are suddenly coming over for dinner. They're easy to assemble and quick to bake, and they have a lovely butterscotchy flavor. Serve the rounds with bowls of vanilla or butter pecan ice cream.

2 cups all-purpose flour
1 teaspoon baking powder
½ teaspoon salt
16 tablespoons (2 sticks) unsalted butter, softened
1 cup packed light brown sugar
1 large egg
1 teaspoon pure vanilla extract
About 36 pecan halves

PREHEAT the oven to 350°F. Line a cookie sheet with parchment paper.

WHISK together the flour, baking powder, and salt in a medium bowl.

USING an electric mixer, beat the butter in a large bowl until creamy. Add the brown sugar and beat until smooth. Beat in the egg and vanilla. With the beaters on low speed, mix in the flour mixture until fully combined.

DROP the dough by level tablespoonfuls onto the prepared sheet, arranging about 2 inches apart. Press a pecan into the center of each cookie. Bake for 11 to 13 minutes or until the edges are golden brown. (The shorter time yields a more tender cookie; with the longer time they're crispier.) Transfer the cookies to a rack to cool.

STORE in an airtight container for up to 3 days, but these cookies are best the day they're baked.

Lace Cookies

MAKES 60 TO 70 COOKIES

Hold these delicate rounds up to the light and you'll see why they're called lace cookies. Thin and brittle, the candylike treats are an elegant finish to any meal.

While very easy to make, these cookies require care *after* baking. If you try to remove them too soon from the cookie sheet, they won't hold their shape. Let them sit for about two minutes to firm up, then use a thin metal spatula to transfer them to a rack to cool.

½	cup pecans
10	tablespoons (1¼ sticks) unsalted butter
1	cup packed dark brown sugar
¼	cup light corn syrup
1	tablespoon heavy (or whipping) cream
1	teaspoon pure vanilla extract
¼	teaspoon salt
¼	cup all-purpose flour
1¼	cups old-fashioned rolled oats

NOTE: This batter freezes well. Transfer it to a plastic container and freeze for up to 2 months.

PREHEAT the oven to 350°F. Line a cookie sheet with parchment paper.

SPREAD the pecans on a small baking sheet and toast for about 7 minutes or until lightly browned and aromatic. Transfer the nuts to a cutting board and chop into small pieces.

MELT the butter in a medium saucepan over low heat. Remove from the heat and, using a wooden spoon, stir in the brown sugar (making sure there are no lumps remaining), corn syrup, cream, vanilla, and salt. Stir in the flour, then mix in the oats and chopped pecans.

DROP the batter by slightly rounded teaspoonfuls, arranging at least 3 inches apart. (These cookies spread until they're paper thin, so don't place them any closer together or make them any larger. You should be able to get 9 cookies per standard cookie sheet.) Bake in the middle of the oven for 6 to 7 minutes or until the cookies are bubbling and golden brown, a little darker around the edges. Transfer the cookie sheet to a rack. (Alternatively, slide the parchment off the sheet and onto a rack.) Wait about 2 minutes for the cookies to firm up. Using a wide metal spatula, carefully transfer the cookies directly onto a rack to cool.

STORE in an airtight container for up to 5 days.

Almond Macaroons

Attention almond lovers: This is your cookie! Chewy, rich, intensely almond, these macaroons couldn't be easier to make, yet are so difficult to stop nibbling on. Go ahead and gild the lily, if you like, and dip the cookies halfway in chocolate for a truly memorable treat.

10	ounces (about 2 full cups) blanched whole almonds
1¼	cups sugar
3	large egg whites
½	teaspoon pure almond extract
6	ounces fine-quality bittersweet chocolate, chopped, optional

Tip: As one batch of macaroons bakes, prepare more rounds on fresh sheets of parchment. When a cookie sheet becomes available, slide the paper with the unbaked macaroons onto the sheet and immediately place in the oven.

PREHEAT the oven to 350°F. Line 1 or 2 cookie sheets with parchment paper.

COMBINE the almonds and ¼ cup of the sugar in a food processor and process until the almonds are finely ground. Add the egg whites and almond extract and process until blended. Add the remaining 1 cup of sugar and process until thoroughly combined, about 15 seconds or until the dough is a thick, sticky paste.

DROP the dough by level tablespoonfuls, arranging about 2 inches apart on the prepared sheet(s). Using a pastry brush lightly moistened with water, brush the tops and sides of the macaroons, gently pressing down on them to form smooth rounds about ½ inch thick and 1¾ inches in diameter.

BAKE for about 15 minutes or until the macaroons are pale golden. They should feel crisp on the outside but still soft inside. (If using 2 cookie sheets, rotate them from top to bottom and front to back about halfway through baking. Remove the sheet(s) from the oven and slide the parchment onto racks.) Cool for about 5 minutes, then use a thin metal spatula to remove the macaroons from the paper. Place on a rack to cool completely.

FOR CHOCOLATE-DIPPED MACAROONS: Melt the chocolate in a metal or glass bowl set over a pan of barely simmering water, stirring frequently, until fully melted. Alternatively, melt it in a microwave-safe bowl in the microwave, using 20- to 30-second bursts at medium power, stirring well after each interval (see page 17). Pour the choco-late into a glass measuring cup or coffee mug. (A container that is nar-row and deep works better than one that is wide and shallow.) Line a baking sheet with wax paper. Dip the macaroons into the melted chocolate to coat half the cookie like a semicircle. Let the excess drip off or gently scrape it off the bottom of the cookie using the rim of the cup. (As the chocolate gets used up, tilt the cup to continue coating the cookies.) Place the macaroons on the wax paper and let stand until the chocolate is completely set. Gently peel the cookies off the paper.

STORE, layered between sheets of wax paper, in an airtight container for up to 5 days. Macaroons without chocolate coating can be frozen for up to 2 months.

Iced Lemon Rounds

MAKES ABOUT *45* COOKIES

These little cakey cookies are a nice surprise. They may not look like much, but the tender rounds are buttery and lemony, and the icing adds a delectable sweet-tartness. To spruce them up for the holidays, you can sprinkle some green or red sugar crystals (or use some of both) on the icing before it sets.

3   cups all-purpose flour
1   teaspoon baking powder
½   teaspoon salt
16 tablespoons (2 sticks) unsalted butter, softened
½   cup granulated sugar
½   cup confectioners' sugar
2   large eggs
2   tablespoons finely grated lemon zest (from about 2 lemons)
¼   cup fresh lemon juice
1   teaspoon pure vanilla extract

LEMON ICING
1   cup confectioners' sugar
1   tablespoon fresh lemon juice
2   teaspoons milk

PREHEAT the oven to 350°F. Line 1 or 2 cookie sheets with parchment paper.

WHISK together the flour, baking powder, and salt in a medium bowl.

USING an electric mixer, beat the butter in a large bowl until creamy. Add the granulated and confectioners' sugars and beat until smooth and creamy. Beat in the eggs, then the lemon zest, lemon juice, and vanilla. With the beaters on low speed, mix in the flour mixture just until fully incorporated. The dough will be thick and a little sticky.

DROP the dough by slightly rounded tablespoonfuls onto the prepared sheet(s), arranging about 2 inches apart. Flatten the mounds slightly with your fingers to about a ½-inch thickness. Bake for about 13 minutes or until pale on top and golden on the bottom. The cookies should feel set but still tender inside. (If using 2 cookie sheets, rotate them from top to bottom and front to back about halfway through baking.) Transfer the cookies to a rack to cool completely.

FOR THE ICING: Whisk the confectioners' sugar, lemon juice, and milk in a small bowl. Spread the icing on the tops of the cookies using a small spreader or a table knife. Let the cookies stand on a rack until the icing sets.

STORE, layered between sheets of wax paper, in an airtight container for up to 1 week.

Coconut Macaroons

Every now and then I get the urge for these moist, chewy treats, so I always keep a can of sweetened condensed milk in the pantry and a bag of coconut in the freezer. I guess you could say that being prepared is worth its weight in macaroons! Chocoholics might want to drizzle melted chocolate over the tops or go hog wild and dip the macaroons right into the chocolate to cover the whole darn thing! (Check out the chocolate-dipping technique on page 32.)

3   cups (about 9 ounces) lightly packed sweetened shredded coconut

½   cup sweetened condensed milk

1   teaspoon pure vanilla extract

1   teaspoon fresh lemon juice

1   large egg white

    Dash of salt

PREHEAT the oven to 350°F. Line a cookie sheet with parchment paper.

COMBINE the coconut, condensed milk, vanilla, and lemon juice in a large bowl.

USING an electric mixer, beat the egg white with the salt in a medium bowl until it holds soft peaks. Fold the white into the coconut mixture.

DROP small mounds of the batter, measuring about 1½ inches in diameter, onto the prepared sheet. Arrange them about 1½ inches apart. With slightly wet fingertips, pinch the mounds to make them a tad narrower and taller, about 1¼ inches in diameter and 1 inch high with a slightly pinched top. Bake for 15 to 17 minutes, rotating the sheet from front to back about two-thirds of the way through baking, or until the macaroons are golden (some coconut shreds on top will be dark brown). Slide the parchment off the cookie sheet and onto a rack. After 5 to 10 minutes, remove the macaroons from the parchment using a thin metal spatula and place them directly on the rack to finish cooling.

STORE in an airtight container for up to 5 days.

Cocoa Meringue Kisses

Containing no flour, butter, or egg yolks, these ethereal kisses are a welcome respite from the holiday season's caloric excesses. Baking the wispy dollops of cocoa-flavored beaten egg whites for the time suggested produces a meringue that is gently crisp on the outside and chewy-soft, almost creamy on the inside.

¾ cup confectioners' sugar

⅓ cup unsweetened (natural) cocoa powder

4 large egg whites, at room temperature

¼ teaspoon cream of tartar

½ cup granulated sugar

½ teaspoon pure vanilla extract

Tip: Meringue making and hot, humid weather don't mix, so save these cookies for cool, dry days.

PREHEAT the oven to 300°F. Line 1 or 2 cookie sheets with parchment paper. If using 2 sheets, make sure to have one oven rack at the bottom of the top third of the oven and one at the top of the lower third, so they're separated by at least 4 inches (see page 3).

SIFT the confectioners' sugar and cocoa through a sieve set over a medium bowl.

USING an electric mixer at medium speed, beat the egg whites and cream of tartar in a large, clean bowl until the whites hold soft peaks. Increase the speed to high and gradually beat in the granulated sugar one tablespoon at a time, until the whites are thick, stiff, and glossy. Beat in the vanilla. Using a rubber spatula, gently fold in the cocoa mixture, making sure it's completely absorbed, but don't get stir-happy or else the whites will deflate too much.

DROP the meringue by slightly rounded tablespoonfuls onto the prepared sheet(s), using a finger of your free hand to push the batter off the spoon. The meringues should be about 1½ inches in diameter and at least 1½ inches high with charming pointy, craggy tops; place them about 2 inches apart on the prepared sheet(s).

BAKE the meringues for 25 minutes or until the outside feels dry but the inside is still soft. (Overbaking will produce meringues that are dry and crisp throughout.) There's no need to rotate the sheets. Carefully slide the parchment off the cookie sheet and onto a rack. When the cookies have cooled, gently peel them off the parchment.

STORE in an airtight container in a cool, dry place (but not in the refrigerator) for up to 3 days, but these are best the day they're made.

Mexican Chocolate Snowballs

MAKES ABOUT 55 COOKIES

These treats belong to the crumbly melt-in-your-mouth cookie family, whose members include the variously named wedding cookies, snowballs, and butterballs. The big difference is that these tender gems are made of chocolate. Their flavor is bittersweet, an exotic blend of cocoa, cinnamon, toasted almonds, and a dash of cayenne pepper.

¾ cup blanched slivered almonds

1¾ cups all-purpose flour

6 tablespoons Dutch-processed cocoa powder

½ teaspoon baking powder

½ teaspoon ground cinnamon

½ teaspoon salt

⅛ teaspoon cayenne pepper, optional (see Note)

16 tablespoons (2 sticks) unsalted butter, softened

½ cup confectioners' sugar, plus about 1¼ cups for coating the cookies

1 large egg yolk

1 teaspoon pure vanilla extract

NOTE: Don't substitute what is sold as "chili powder" because this is a blend containing other spices and garlic.

PREHEAT the oven to 325°F. Line 2 cookie sheets with parchment paper.

SPREAD the almonds on a small baking sheet and toast in the oven for 6 to 8 minutes or until golden. Transfer them to a cutting board; when cool enough to handle, chop fine. Maintain the oven temperature.

WHISK together the flour, cocoa, baking powder, cinnamon, salt, and cayenne pepper, if using, in a medium bowl.

USING an electric mixer, beat the butter in a large bowl until creamy. Add ½ cup of the confectioners' sugar and beat until fully blended. Beat in the egg yolk, then the vanilla. With the beaters on low speed, mix in the flour mixture until fully incorporated. Mix in the almonds.

DROP the dough by rounded teaspoonfuls onto the prepared sheets, arranging about 1½ inches apart. Bake for 15 to 16 minutes, rotating the sheets from top to bottom and front to back halfway through baking, or until the tops are semifirm to the touch but the inside still feels tender. Carefully transfer the cookies to a rack to cool for 5 minutes.

PLACE the remaining 1¼ cups of confectioners' sugar in a shallow bowl. While the cookies are still warm, gently roll them in the sugar, then transfer them to a rack to cool. Just before serving or storing, recoat the cookies with sugar.

STORE, layered between sheets of wax paper, in an airtight container for up to 10 days; or freeze for up to 2 months.

Rolled Cookies

Tips FOR MAKING ROLLED COOKIES

- The more holiday cookie cutters you have, the merrier your cookie plates will be! Using the rim of a glass to stamp out circles should be your last resort because it lacks holiday pizzazz. Look for festive cutters in kitchen stores and arts and crafts stores, at flea markets, and online.

- Chill the dough for the time specified in the recipe so it can rest and firm up before rolling. If chilled for a longer period, however, these doughs will become very hard. Just let them sit at room temperature for as long as 30 to 60 minutes to soften.

- Work with the amount of dough specified in the recipe and keep the remainder in the fridge. Rolling out too much at one time will cause it to soften, and you will end up with scraps that have to be reworked.

- Always work on a clean surface that is large enough to hold the rolled-out dough. Lightly flouring the space helps prevent the dough from sticking, but be wary of using too much flour, as the dough will toughen and the flavor and texture of the baked cookies will suffer.

- The dough must be the right temperature and consistency to roll out: if it's too cold, it will be arm-breaking to roll; too warm or too soft and it will stick to the work surface or rolling pin (or both) and you'll end up using too much flour to make it manageable. Rolling dough on or between sheets of wax paper allows you to

slide it onto a cookie sheet and refrigerate it for 10 to 15 minutes to firm as needed.

- Roll the dough to the thickness recommended in the recipe for the cookies to bake evenly in the time suggested. Thinner cookies will brown faster and thicker cookies may end up underbaked.

- Stamp out shapes close together to reduce scraps. You can reroll the scraps a few times, but some doughs may start to toughen from being overworked and overfloured. The doughs for Dutch Spice Cookies and Gingerbread People are very forgiving and those scraps can be re-rolled a number of times. When scraps become too soft to work with, press them together, wrap in plastic, and refrigerate the dough until it's firm enough to roll again. Use a thin metal spatula to transfer cutout shapes to the cookie sheet.

TO MAKE COOKIE ORNAMENTS:

While the unbaked cookies are lying flat on a parchment-lined cookie sheet, use the tip of a metal skewer to pierce holes at the tops of the shapes. Enlarge the hole by making tiny circles with the skewer tip until the opening is at least $\frac{1}{4}$ inch in diameter. (The hole will shrink during baking so it must start out larger than needed.) After the cookies have baked and cooled, reinforce the hole, if needed, by gently twirling the skewer in the hole. After the cookies have been decorated and the icing has completely dried, slip a thin ribbon or colored string through each hole to hang the cookies from a tree or fireplace mantel.

Cornmeal Currant Cookies

MAKES ABOUT *40* COOKIES

These buttery rounds have a delicate crunch from cornmeal and subtle flavor from currants that have been soaked in port, a sweet fortified wine. Serve the cookies with wine-poached pears for a sophisticated dessert.

¾	cup currants
¼	cup good-quality port
2¼	cups all-purpose flour
1	cup fine yellow cornmeal (don't use coarse polenta)
1	teaspoon baking powder
½	teaspoon salt
16	tablespoons (2 sticks) unsalted butter, softened
1	cup sugar
1	large egg

COOKIE CUTTER NEEDED: 2½-inch round or square, preferably with fluted or scalloped edges

COMBINE the currants and port in a small bowl; let sit at room temperature for 30 minutes.

WHISK together the flour, cornmeal, baking powder, and salt in a medium bowl.

USING an electric mixer, beat the butter in a large bowl until creamy. Add the sugar and beat well until fully blended. Beat in the egg. With the beaters on low speed, mix in the currants and port, then mix in the flour mixture just until fully combined. Divide the dough in half. Press each half into a disk, wrap separately in plastic wrap, and refrigerate until firm enough to roll out, at least 2 hours.

PREHEAT the oven to 375°F. Have ready an ungreased cookie sheet.

WORKING with one disk at a time, roll it out on a lightly floured surface about ¼ inch thick. Using the cutter, stamp out cookies close together and place them on the cookie sheet about 1½ inches apart. Reroll the scraps and repeat the process, stamping out cookies and arranging them on the cookie sheet. Bake for about 12 minutes or until the cookies are lightly golden, though a little browner around the edges. Transfer the cookies to a rack to cool.

STORE in an airtight container for up to 1 week; or freeze for up to 2 months. To recrisp cookies that have been frozen, heat on a baking sheet in a 375°F oven for about 3 minutes.

Dutch Spice Cookies

MAKES ABOUT 55 COOKIES (depending on the size of the cookie cutters)

Thin, crisp spice cookies are ubiquitous at Christmastime in most northern European countries. One particularly popular variety is called *speculaas* in the Netherlands, *speculoos* in Belgium, and *Spekulatius* in Germany. Believed to be named for the Latin word *speculum*, meaning "mirror," these cookies reflect the image of the specially designed wooden molds that the dough is pressed into. Cookies in the shape of a windmill are probably one of the more familiar designs, but you don't need fancy molds to make these treats. Any shape will do, although I like to use a fluted, diamond-shaped cutter that measures approximately 2 × 3 inches.

2¼	cups all-purpose flour
½	teaspoon baking powder
¼	teaspoon salt
1	teaspoon ground cinnamon
¼	teaspoon freshly grated nutmeg
¼	teaspoon ground ginger
¼	teaspoon ground allspice (or cloves)
8	tablespoons (1 stick) unsalted butter, softened
1	cup packed dark brown sugar
1	large egg
1	teaspoon grated lemon zest
	Egg wash: 1 egg white whisked with 2 teaspoons water until frothy
¾	cup sliced almonds

COOKIE CUTTER NEEDED: diamond, square, or round measuring about 2½ inches in diameter

Whisk together the flour, baking powder, salt, cinnamon, nutmeg, ginger, and allspice in a medium bowl.

Using an electric mixer, beat the butter and brown sugar in a large bowl until creamy. Beat in the egg, then the lemon zest. With the beaters on low speed, mix in the flour mixture until thoroughly combined. Gather the dough into a ball, then divide it in half. Shape each half into a disk and wrap separately in plastic. Refrigerate for at least 1 hour.

PREHEAT the oven to 350°F. Line a cookie sheet with parchment paper.

WORKING with one disk at a time, roll out the dough on a lightly floured surface to a ¼-inch thickness. Using the cutter, stamp out diamonds (or other shapes), arranging them about 1½ inches apart on the prepared sheet. Reroll the scraps. Using a pastry brush, lightly brush the egg wash over the tops of the cookies. Press a few almonds onto the center of each cookie.

BAKE for 13 to 14 minutes or until the cookies are slightly browned around the edges and the almonds are golden. (The cookies will crisp up as they cool.) Transfer the cookies to a rack to cool.

STORE in an airtight container for up to 2 weeks; or freeze for up to 3 months.

Sugar Cookies

MAKES *35* TO *45* COOKIES (depending on the size of the cookie cutters)

For holiday bakers and their hungry fans, the simple sugar cookie decorated in festive style perhaps most vividly captures the spirit of Christmas. To make these special treats, you'll need to dig out your stash of holiday cookie cutters and assorted decorating paraphernalia, whip up a batch of Royal Icing (recipe follows), and turn up the Christmas carols. Round up a few elves to help and you might catch yourself whistling as you work.

2¼   cups all-purpose flour
1   teaspoon baking powder
½   teaspoon salt
12   tablespoons (1½ sticks) unsalted butter, softened
¾   cup sugar
1   large egg
1   teaspoon pure vanilla extract
½   teaspoon finely grated lemon zest

DECORATIONS

Colored sugar crystals, coarse sugar, nonpareils

COOKIE CUTTERS NEEDED: all kinds of holiday shapes

WHISK together the flour, baking powder, and salt in a medium bowl.

USING an electric mixer, beat the butter in a large bowl until creamy. Add the sugar and beat well until fluffy, 1 to 2 minutes. Beat in the egg, then the vanilla and lemon zest. With the beaters on low speed, mix in the flour mixture until fully incorporated and the dough starts to come together. Using your hands or a rubber spatula, gather the dough into a ball. Divide the dough in half, place each half on a sheet of plastic wrap, press into a disk, and wrap. Refrigerate the dough for at least 2 hours or until firm. (The dough can be refrigerated for up to 3 days or frozen for up to 2 months.)

PREHEAT the oven to 325°F. Line 1 or 2 cookie sheets with parchment paper.

REMOVE one disk of dough from the refrigerator and let it sit at room temperature for about 10 minutes or until softened slightly. Roll the dough between two sheets of wax paper (see Note) to an even ¼-inch thickness. (When rolling dough between sheets of wax paper it's easy to roll it too thin, so lift the top sheet occasionally and measure the thickness of the dough. Also check to make sure the paper isn't creased; if it is, smooth the paper and roll out any wrinkles in the dough.) Peel off the top sheet of wax paper and stamp out cookies close together to minimize scraps. Using a thin metal spatula, transfer the shapes to the prepared sheet(s), arranging them about 1½ inches apart. Gather the scraps into a ball, wrap in plastic wrap, and refrigerate; reroll a few times. Repeat with the remaining dough.

IF applying decorations before baking, sprinkle the cookies with sugars and/or nonpareils. (Press gently on the nonpareils so they don't roll off.) Leave the cookies undecorated if you want to apply icing and decorations after baking. (See below.)

BAKE the cookies for 12 to 15 minutes or until the edges are lightly golden. The cookies shouldn't color much. (If using 2 sheets, rotate them from top to bottom and front to back halfway through baking.) Carefully transfer the cookies to a rack to cool completely.

STORE plain or sugared cookies in an airtight container for up to 10 days. Undecorated cookies can be frozen for up to 2 months.

NOTE: Some sugar cookie doughs can be difficult to work with, turning soft and sticky as you're rolling or stamping them. I think you'll find this dough easy to assemble and firm enough to roll and cut into shapes. On a warm day, though, it, too, can become soft, so I recommend lightly flouring the wax paper before rolling out the dough and then refrigerating the dough on a cookie sheet to firm it before stamping out cookies.

Tip: Have the next batch of cookies ready to go on a clean sheet of parchment placed on a cooled cookie sheet; refrigerate until baking time.

See photograph of Sugar Cookies on page 14.

Royal Icing (For iced and decorated sugar cookies)

2¼ cups (about 9 ounces)
confectioners' sugar
1 tablespoon plus 1 teaspoon
dried egg whites (meringue
powder), such as Just Whites
4 to 5 tablespoons warm water
Food coloring liquids, gels, or
pastes

DECORATIONS
Colored sugar crystals,
coarse sugar, nonpareils,
mini candies, chocolate and
rainbow sprinkles, sweetened
shredded coconut

USING an electric mixer set on low speed, beat the confectioners' sugar, dried egg whites, and 4 tablespoons of warm water in a large bowl until blended. Increase the speed to medium and beat until the icing is thick and glossy, 3 to 4 minutes. If the icing appears very thick, add a few drops of water. If the icing seems thin, add a little more confectioners' sugar.

SPOON the icing into small bowls and tint with food coloring to the desired shades, stirring completely. (Store icings in small, airtight plastic containers at room temperature for up to 3 days; stir well before using.)

FOR PIPING: Spoon the icing, which should be fairly thick for this purpose, into a squeeze bottle (see Tip) or pastry bag fitted with a small round decorating tip. Carefully pipe the icing around the edge of the cookie or in any decorative design. Allow piping to set before filling in the outline or using another color.

FOR PAINTING: Thin the icing with a few drops of water to make icing paint for filling in outlined shapes. Using a small paintbrush, spread the icing on the cookie, going all the way to the piped outline. Before the icing sets, apply decorations as desired. Let the icing set completely before storing the cookies.

STORE iced and decorated cookies, layered between sheets of wax paper, in an airtight container for up to 2 weeks.

Tip: Using a plastic squeeze bottle is easy. Spoon the icing into the bottle, screw on the top, and turn the bottle upside down. Holding your finger over the hole, shake the icing down into the nozzle. Squeeze the bottle, applying steady pressure, to pipe icing onto cookies. If the icing hardly budges, thin it with a few drops of milk or water. Store the bottle upside down in a coffee mug (or other sturdy container) while you're using it and for up to a few days. If the hole becomes clogged, insert a toothpick to clean it out.

Sugar Cookies with Stained Glass

MAKES 35 TO 45 COOKIES (depending on the size of the cookie cutters)

Any sugar cookie can be given a window of stained glass. The "glass" comes from crushed hard candies that melt in the oven, creating a translucent colored pane. The "window" is cut out of the cookie using small (1-inch) cutters; or, if you have a steady hand, you can cut out shapes using the tip of a knife.

About 4 ounces hard candies, in various colors and flavors

1 recipe Sugar Cookies (page 46)

Granulated or colored sugar, optional

COOKIE CUTTERS NEEDED: 2½- to 3-inch shapes for the cookies and 1-inch-diameter cutouts, such as fluted rounds, hearts, and stars, for the "windows"

PREHEAT the oven to 350°F. Line 1 or 2 cookie sheets with parchment paper.

PLACE like-colored candies in small plastic bags. Seal the bags and crush the candy with the smooth side of a meat mallet or hammer until the candy is powdery. Keeping the colors separate, place the candy into small cups.

ROLL out the sugar cookie dough and stamp it into shapes as directed on pages 46 to 47. Stamp out a window in each cookie using the 1-inch cutter. Using a thin metal spatula, carefully transfer the cookies to the prepared sheet(s), arranging them about 1½ inches apart. Remove the small cutout if it didn't already come out with the cutter. Reroll the cutouts as scraps.

USING the smallest, pointiest spoon you have, such as a demitasse spoon, carefully fill the windows with the powdered candy, filling almost up to the height of the cookie. Try not to get any candy on top of the cookie. Sprinkle the cookies lightly with granulated or colored sugar, if desired.

BAKE the cookies for 10 to 11 minutes or until the edges are lightly golden and the candy has melted and appears translucent. (If using 2 sheets, rotate them from top to bottom and front to back about half-way through baking.) Transfer the cookie sheet(s) to a rack and let the cookies cool on the sheets. Don't attempt to remove the cookies from the parchment too soon or the candy will stick. Once the candy has set, transfer the cookies to a rack to cool completely.

STORE, layered between sheets of wax paper, in an airtight container for up to 10 days.

See photograph of Sugar Cookies with Stained Glass on page 13.

Walnut Stars

This cookie dough is conveniently made in a food processor, just as you might make pastry dough. The stars have a delicate crunch and lovely earthy-nutty flavor from toasted walnuts. (Using toasted nuts is important, so don't skip this step!) The chocolate drizzle is icing on the cake . . . I mean cookie.

1	cup (about 4 ounces) walnuts
¼	cup granulated sugar
1½	cups all-purpose flour
½	cup confectioners' sugar
½	teaspoon baking powder
¼	teaspoon salt
8	tablespoons (1 stick) chilled unsalted butter, cut into 8 slices
1	large egg yolk
1	teaspoon pure vanilla extract
1 to 2	tablespoons cold water

CHOCOLATE DRIZZLE

3	ounces bittersweet or semisweet chocolate, chopped

COOKIE CUTTERS NEEDED: star shapes that measure from about 1¾ to 2½ inches across the "arms"

PREHEAT the oven to 325°F. Spread the walnuts in a single layer on a small baking sheet. Toast in the oven for about 8 minutes or just until you start to smell them. Remove from the oven and cool to room temperature. Turn off the oven.

PULSE the cooled, toasted walnuts and the granulated sugar in a food processor until the nuts are finely chopped (not quite finely ground). Transfer the mixture to a small bowl.

ADD the flour, confectioners' sugar, baking powder, and salt to the food processor. Pulse once to combine. Add the butter and pulse a few times until it's chopped into tiny bits. Add the walnut mixture and pulse twice to combine. Add the egg yolk, vanilla, and 1 tablespoon of water and process just until the dough feels moist when pinched. Add ½ to 1 tablespoon more water, as needed, and pulse a few more times until the dough just starts to clump together. Turn the dough out onto a sheet of plastic wrap and gather into a ball. Press into a disk shape, wrap in plastic, and refrigerate until firm enough to roll out, at least 1 hour.

PREHEAT the oven to 350°F. Line a cookie sheet with parchment paper.

ROLL out the dough on a lightly floured surface to a ¼-inch thickness. Use star cutters to stamp out cookies, arranging them about 1½ inches apart on the prepared sheet. Reroll the scraps. Bake the cookies for 11 to 12 minutes or until light golden. Transfer to a rack to cool completely.

FOR THE CHOCOLATE DRIZZLE: Melt the chocolate in a microwave-safe glass measuring cup or bowl in the microwave in 20- to 30-second bursts on medium power, stirring after each interval, until melted and smooth. Let cool at room temperature for a few minutes. Place the cookies close together, but not touching, on racks set over wax paper. Pour the chocolate into a small plastic bag or squeeze bottle. If using a bag, seal it and make a tiny cut in one corner. Working quickly, drizzle the chocolate in a zigzag pattern to make diagonal lines over the stars. Let the chocolate set completely before storing the cookies.

STORE, layered between sheets of wax paper, in an airtight container for up to 1 week.

Gingerbread People

MAKES 35 TO 45 COOKIES (depending on the size of the cookie cutters)

I used to think gingerbread people were mostly for decorating and looking at, but not for eating. Now I think they're as yummy to eat as they are fun to make. The texture is light and crisp, and the spice is just right. Best of all, the cookies aren't too sweet. This way, the kids can decorate the little people with icing and all kinds of candy and not go into sugar shock!

3	cups all-purpose flour
2	teaspoons ground ginger
1	teaspoon ground cinnamon
¼	teaspoon ground cloves
1	teaspoon baking soda
¼	teaspoon salt
8	tablespoons (1 stick) unsalted butter, softened
¾	cup packed dark brown sugar
1	large egg
½	cup molasses

Confectioners' Sugar Icing (recipe follows)

NOTE: For instructions on making gingerbread cookie ornaments, see page 42.

COOKIE CUTTERS NEEDED: "people" from 3 to 5 inches tall

WHISK together the flour, ginger, cinnamon, cloves, baking soda, and salt in a medium bowl.

USING an electric mixer, beat the butter and brown sugar in a large bowl until creamy. Beat in the egg, then the molasses. With the beaters on low speed, mix in the flour mixture until incorporated and the dough starts to clump together. Gather the dough into a ball, then divide it in half. Flatten each half into a disk and wrap separately in plastic wrap. Chill for at least 2 hours or until firm enough to roll out.

PREHEAT the oven to 350°F. Line 2 cookie sheets with parchment paper.

WORKING with one disk at a time, roll it out on a well-floured surface to a scant ¼-inch thickness. (Sprinkle the rolling pin with flour if the dough sticks to it.) Use assorted "people" cutters to stamp out cookies. Using a thin metal spatula, transfer the cookies to the prepared sheets, arranging them about 1½ inches apart. Gather the scraps into a ball, chill the dough as necessary, and reroll a few times.

BAKE the cookies for about 11 minutes, rotating the sheets from top to bottom and front to back halfway through baking, or until the edges appear slightly browned. Let the cookies rest on the sheets for a few minutes to firm up, then carefully transfer them to a rack to cool completely before decorating.

STORE undecorated cookies in an airtight container for up to 3 weeks.

Confectioners' Sugar Icing

6 cups confectioners' sugar
6 to 8 tablespoons milk
2 tablespoons fresh lemon juice
Food colorings, optional

DECORATIONS

Colored and coarse sugars, chocolate and rainbow sprinkles, multicolor nonpareils, Red Hots and other mini-candies, sweetened shredded coconut, raisins

PLACE the confectioners' sugar in a large bowl. Whisk in 6 tablespoons of the milk and the lemon juice. Add more milk as needed, but keep in mind that the icing must be thick enough to pipe.

IF using food coloring, divide the icing among a few small bowls. Add the food coloring by drops, tinting the icing to the desired shade.

SPOON the icing into a squeeze bottle (see Tip on page 48) or a pastry bag fitted with a small round decorating tip. Pipe the icing around the edge of the cookie or in any pattern desired. To glaze a cookie with icing or paint inside a piped outline, thin the icing slightly with milk and then spread the icing on the cookie with a small paintbrush. Before the icing dries, decorate with assorted sugars and candies. (Wet icing acts as the glue.) Let the icing set completely before storing the cookies.

STORE iced and decorated cookies, layered between sheets of wax paper, in an airtight container for up to 10 days.

Slice and Bake Cookies

$Tips$ FOR MAKING SLICE AND BAKE COOKIES

Life is good when there are logs of cookie dough in the freezer. That way, you can make cookies whenever you want to.

- Slice and bake cookies, also called refrigerator, icebox, or freezer cookies, usually contain enough butter for the dough to freeze well for a few months and then soften to slicing consistency fairly quickly—in about 30 to 45 minutes—at room temperature.

- When forming logs of dough, try to make them the suggested length and diameter so the cookies will all be the same size when they're sliced and baked and so that you'll end up with the indicated yield. To form a log, first squeeze and shape the dough into a log a tad shorter and fatter than the recommended size. Then roll the log back and forth on your work surface to form a smooth cylinder of the correct measurements.

- Double wrap all logs: Roll up the dough in plastic wrap, twisting the ends of the plastic to enclose the dough, then roll it up in foil to create a sturdy, freezer-proof package. In general, you can refrigerate the logs for up to 3 days or freeze them for up to 3 months. Make sure the logs are lying flat in the freezer and that nothing is poking into them or you'll end up with crooked logs and misshapen cookies.

- When you're ready to bake, bring the log to slicing temperature, which is cold and firm but not rock hard. You won't get neat slices if the dough is either too soft or frozen solid. (The baking times in the recipes assume that the dough is cold when it goes into the oven.) Slice the dough with a thin-bladed knife to the thickness indicated in the recipe so the cookies bake evenly in the time suggested. Every 4 or 5 slices, give the log a quarter turn to prevent the bottom from getting squashed. Pop the log back into the freezer for about 15 minutes if it softens too much during slicing.

Ginger Coins

With a delicate spice and delightful crunch, these thin ginger snaps are as perfect with ice cream as they are with a cup of tea. If you like your snaps snappier, which I highly recommend, add the larger amount of black pepper.

2¼ cups all-purpose flour

1 teaspoon baking soda

¼ teaspoon salt

1 tablespoon ground ginger

½ teaspoon ground cinnamon

¼ teaspoon ground cloves

⅛ to ¼ teaspoon freshly ground black pepper

12 tablespoons (1½ sticks) unsalted butter, softened

¾ cup granulated sugar

½ cup packed dark brown sugar

1 large egg

1 teaspoon pure vanilla extract

WHISK together the flour, baking soda, salt, ginger, cinnamon, cloves, and pepper in a medium bowl.

USING an electric mixer, beat the butter in a large bowl until creamy. Add the granulated and brown sugars and beat until fully blended. Beat in the egg, then the vanilla. With the beaters on low speed, mix in the flour mixture until incorporated and the dough starts to clump together. Gather the dough into a ball, then divide it in half.

WORKING with one half of the dough at a time, shape it into a narrow log, rolling it back and forth on a work surface until it's a smooth cylinder about 11 inches long and 1¼ inches in diameter. Roll up the dough in a sheet of plastic wrap and secure with a layer of foil. Repeat with the remaining dough. Refrigerate for at least 2 hours or until very firm. (Or freeze the logs for up to 3 months.)

PREHEAT the oven to 350°F. Line a cookie sheet with parchment paper.

WORKING with one log at a time, cut the dough into ¼-inch-thick slices, arranging them about 1½ inches apart on the prepared sheet. Bake for 11 minutes or until the cookies are gently browned. (They'll crisp up more as they cool.) Transfer the cookies to a rack to cool.

STORE in an airtight container for up to 2 weeks.

Eggnog Cookies

Capturing the flavors of eggnog, a traditional Christmastime beverage, in a cookie is easy. These rich, buttery rounds hint of nutmeg and cinnamon and are topped with a spoonful of rum icing. A dusting of freshly grated nutmeg adds to the holiday motif.

1¾	cups all-purpose flour
½	teaspoon freshly grated nutmeg
½	teaspoon ground cinnamon
¼	teaspoon salt
16	tablespoons (2 sticks) unsalted butter, softened
½	cup granulated sugar
⅓	cup confectioners' sugar
1	large egg yolk

RUM ICING

1	cup confectioners' sugar
2½ to 3	tablespoons light rum
1	whole nutmeg, for grating on top of the cookies

WHISK together the flour, nutmeg, cinnamon, and salt in a medium bowl.

USING an electric mixer, beat the butter in a large bowl until creamy. Add the granulated and confectioners' sugars and beat until thoroughly blended and velvety. Beat in the egg yolk. With the beaters on low speed, mix in the flour mixture just until thoroughly combined and the dough starts to come together. Gather the dough into a ball, then divide it in half.

WORKING with one half of the dough at a time, place it on a lightly floured surface. Use your hands to shape it into a log and then roll it back and forth to form a smooth cylinder about 6 to 7 inches long and 1¾ inches in diameter. Wrap up the log in plastic wrap and secure with a layer of foil. Repeat with the remaining dough. Refrigerate for at least 4 hours or until very firm. (The dough can be refrigerated for up to 3 days or frozen for up to 3 months.)

PREHEAT the oven to 350°F. Line a cookie sheet with parchment paper.

WORKING with one log at a time, use a sharp knife to cut the dough into slices between ¼ and ⅓ inch thick. Place the rounds on the prepared sheet, arranging them about 2 inches apart. Bake for about 13 minutes or until the cookies are pale golden, a little browner around the edges. Transfer the cookies to a rack to cool completely.

FOR THE RUM ICING: Whisk the confectioners' sugar and 2½ tablespoons of the rum in a small bowl until smooth. Add a little more rum as needed to get a spreadable, slightly thin consistency. Spoon ½ teaspoon of icing onto the center of each cookie and spread it with the back of the spoon to form about a 1¼-inch circle. Place the cookies on a rack, and while the icing is still wet, grate a little nutmeg over the tops of the cookies. Let stand until the icing sets completely.

STORE, in layers separated by wax paper, in an airtight container for up to 10 days.

Tip: You can find whole nutmeg, the small, brown, leathery-looking seed of the nutmeg tree, in jars at specialty food stores and some supermarkets. I always use a Microplane grater to grate nutmeg. The fine particles are downy soft and intensely floral.

Pinwheel Cookies

MAKES 60 TO 70 COOKIES

Did you eat these when you were a child? Did you work around the cookie eating whichever ring—chocolate or vanilla—was on the outside and then work your way toward the center? These spirals, called *Schnecken* in German, meaning "snails," require a little more attention than most cookies because you have to roll out two different doughs and then roll them up together like a jelly roll. But they're fun to eat, a pleasure to give, and look special on holiday plates.

2	ounces unsweetened chocolate, chopped
3¼	cups all-purpose flour
1	teaspoon baking powder
½	teaspoon salt
16	tablespoons (2 sticks) unsalted butter, softened
1½	cups sugar
2	large eggs
1½	teaspoons pure vanilla extract
	About 1 tablespoon unsweetened cocoa powder, for rolling out the chocolate dough

MELT the chocolate in a microwave-safe bowl in the microwave at medium power for 20-second bursts, stirring after each interval, and stopping before it is fully melted. Stir to melt fully. Cool slightly.

WHISK together the flour, baking powder, and salt in a medium bowl.

USING an electric mixer, beat the butter in a large bowl until creamy. Add the sugar and beat well until fluffy. Beat in the eggs, then the vanilla. With the beaters on low speed, mix in the flour mixture until fully combined and the dough comes together. Divide the dough in half and place each half on a sheet of plastic wrap. Weigh each portion on a kitchen scale to make sure they're roughly the same size. If one is slightly heavier, use that for the vanilla dough; press it into a disk, wrap in the plastic, and refrigerate.

RETURN the other half of the dough to the mixing bowl and pour the melted chocolate over it. With the beaters on low speed, mix in the chocolate just until combined. Press the dough into a disk and wrap in plastic. Refrigerate both disks for at least 1 hour or until firm enough to roll out.

REMOVE both the vanilla and chocolate doughs from the fridge. Cut 2 sheets of wax paper about 18 inches long. Sprinkle one sheet with flour. (Don't be stingy with the flour or the dough might stick to the paper when you're rolling it up into a spiral.) Roll out the vanilla dough on the paper into a rectangle about 16 inches long and 10 inches wide. Use a bench scraper or knife to trim away excess dough, then press the trimmings onto areas that need it. Slide the wax paper with the dough on it onto a cookie sheet and refrigerate.

SPRINKLE the second sheet of wax paper with a little cocoa. Roll out the chocolate dough, sprinkling the top with cocoa if the rolling pin sticks to it, to form the same size rectangle, about 16 inches long and 10 inches wide.

REMOVE the vanilla dough from the refrigerator and place it (still on the sheet of wax paper) on a clean work surface. Brush the dough very lightly with water. Carefully invert the chocolate dough onto the vanilla dough, using the wax paper as a guide to position it evenly. Gently run a rolling pin over the top to seal the two doughs together. Peel the wax paper off the chocolate dough.

PLACE the dough horizontally in front of you. Starting with the long side at the bottom, use the wax paper (under the vanilla dough) as a guide to roll up the dough into a spiral, making it as tight as possible. Keep rolling to the end. If the chocolate dough is protruding, slice off the excess.

CUT the roll in half to make two 8-inch-long logs. Wrap each log snugly in plastic wrap, then wrap in a layer of foil. Refrigerate the logs for at least 3 hours or until very firm. (Or freeze for up to 2 months.)

PREHEAT the oven to 350°F. Line 2 cookie sheets with parchment paper.

WORKING with one log at a time, cut the dough into ¼-inch-thick slices and place about 1½ inches apart on the prepared sheets. Every few slices, give the log a quarter turn to prevent the bottom from getting squashed. Refrigerate or freeze the log if it softens too much during slic-ing. Bake the cookies for 11 to 14 minutes, rotating the sheets from top to bottom and front to back about halfway through baking, or until the vanilla dough is lightly golden. Transfer the cookies to a rack to cool.

STORE in an airtight container for up to 1 week; or freeze for up to 2 months.

Chocolate Espresso Wafers

MAKES ABOUT *50* COOKIES

For the folks who like their chocolate cookies straight up and unadorned, these crisp wafers have a deep, dark chocolaty flavor with a hint of coffee. They hardly need embellishment, but sandwiching a layer of vanilla ice cream between two rounds makes an awfully nice dessert.

1 ½ cups all-purpose flour
¾ cup unsweetened (natural) cocoa powder
1 ½ tablespoons instant espresso powder, such as Medaglia D'Oro
½ teaspoon baking soda
¼ teaspoon salt
12 tablespoons (1 ½ sticks) unsalted butter, softened
1 cup sugar
1 large egg
1 teaspoon pure vanilla extract

WHISK together the flour, cocoa, espresso powder, baking soda, and salt in a medium bowl.

USING an electric mixer, beat the butter in a large bowl until creamy. Beat in the sugar and mix until fully blended. Beat in the egg, then the vanilla. With the beaters on low speed, mix in the flour mixture until fully incorporated and the dough starts to come together. The dough will be thick and heavy. Gather the dough into a ball, then divide it in half.

WORKING with one half of the dough at a time, place it on a clean work surface and shape it into a log, rolling it back and forth to form a smooth cylinder about 7 ½ inches long and 1 ¾ inches in diameter. (The dough will feel like Play-Doh!) Wrap up the log in plastic wrap and secure with a layer of foil. Repeat with the remaining dough. Refrigerate or freeze until very firm. (The dough can be refrigerated for up to 3 days or frozen for up to 3 months.)

PREHEAT the oven to 350°F. Line a cookie sheet with parchment paper.

WORKING with one log at a time, use a thin, sharp knife to cut the dough into ¼-inch-thick slices, arranging them about 2 inches apart on the prepared sheet. Bake for 12 to 13 minutes or until the cookies feel almost firm to the touch. (They'll crisp up as they cool.) Don't overbake or else the chocolate will taste and smell burnt. Transfer the cookies to a rack to cool.

STORE in an airtight container for up to 10 days; or freeze for up to 2 months.

Pecan Sandies

MAKES ABOUT 45 COOKIES

Just like the old-fashioned favorite of the same name, this buttery cookie is really a classic French sablé (pronounced *SAH-blay* and meaning "sandy") made with finely chopped toasted pecans. Make the dough ahead, freeze it, and you'll always be able to whip up a batch of these memorable treats when guests are coming.

¾	cup pecans (about 3 ounces), toasted and cooled
16	tablespoons (2 sticks) unsalted butter, softened
¾	cup sugar
1	large egg yolk
1	teaspoon pure vanilla extract
¼	teaspoon salt
1¾	cups all-purpose flour

PROCESS the toasted pecans in a food processor until finely chopped (but not quite finely ground) or chop them fine using a chef's knife.

USING an electric mixer, beat the butter in a large bowl until creamy. Add the sugar and beat until fully blended. Beat in the egg yolk, then the vanilla and salt. With the beaters on low speed, mix in the pecans, then mix in the flour just until fully combined and the dough starts to come together. Using your hands or a rubber spatula, gather the dough into a ball, then divide it in half.

WORKING with one half of the dough at a time on a lightly floured surface, shape it into a log, rolling it back and forth to form a smooth cylinder about 8½ inches long and 1½ to 1¾ inches in diameter. Roll up the log in plastic wrap and secure with a layer of foil. Repeat with the remaining dough. Refrigerate for at least 4 hours or until very firm. (The logs can be refrigerated for up to 3 days or frozen for up to 3 months.)

PREHEAT the oven to 350°F. Line a cookie sheet with parchment paper.

WORKING with one log at a time, cut the dough into ⅓-inch-thick slices, arranging them about 1½ inches apart on the prepared sheet. Bake for 15 to 17 minutes or until golden around the edges. Transfer the cookies to a rack to cool.

STORE in an airtight container for up to 10 days.

SLICE AND BAKE COOKIES 67

Toasted Coconut Sablés

MAKES ABOUT 45 COOKIES

I've added coconut to these rich, buttery sablés—both inside and out. Pair them with a luscious tropical fruit salad and you'll have a convenient cure for the winter blahs.

½ cup lightly packed sweetened shredded coconut, plus about ¾ cup for topping the cookies

16 tablespoons (2 sticks) unsalted butter, softened

⅔ cup sugar

1 large egg yolk

½ teaspoon natural coconut flavoring (see Note)

½ teaspoon pure vanilla extract

2 cups all-purpose flour

¼ teaspoon salt

NOTE: While the coconut flavoring isn't absolutely necessary, the cookies won't taste as coconutty without it.

PLACE ½ cup of coconut in a small, heavy skillet and set over moderate heat. Toast the coconut, stirring often, for about 6 minutes or until the shreds are mostly golden. Immediately spread the coconut out on a cutting board to stop the cooking; chop into small bits with a chef's knife.

USING an electric mixer, beat the butter in a large bowl until creamy. Add the sugar and beat until fully blended. Beat in the egg yolk, then the coconut flavoring and vanilla. With the beaters on low speed, mix in the toasted coconut, flour, and salt just until combined. The dough will be crumbly but will feel moist when pinched. Gather the dough into a ball, then divide it in half.

WORKING with one half of the dough at a time on a lightly floured surface, form it into a rough log shape, and then roll it back and forth to form a smooth cylinder about 9 inches long and 1¼ to 1½ inches in diameter. Roll up the log in plastic wrap and secure with a layer of foil. Repeat with the remaining dough. Refrigerate the logs for a few hours or freeze until firm.

PREHEAT the oven to 350°F. Line a cookie sheet with parchment paper.

WORKING with one log at a time, cut the dough into ⅓-inch-thick slices, arranging them about 1½ inches apart on the prepared sheet. Press about ¾ teaspoon of the remaining shredded coconut on top of each cookie. Bake for 14 to 16 minutes or until the coconut topping is nicely golden. Carefully transfer the cookies to a rack to cool.

STORE, layered between sheets of wax paper, in an airtight container for up to 10 days.

Hand-Shaped Cookies

Pecan Butterballs

Tender, crumbly, melt-in-your-mouth cookies appear in many international cuisines: they might be Greek *kourabiedes*, Mexican wedding cookies, Russian tea cakes, or what are more commonly known as snowballs or butterballs. The recipes rely on at least one cup of butter, finely chopped or ground nuts, and a generous coating of snow-white powdered sugar (hence the reference to snow or weddings in some of their names). I grew up calling them "pecan butterballs," which perfectly describes these chubby, buttery, pecan-studded treats.

16	tablespoons (2 sticks) unsalted butter, softened
½	cup confectioners' sugar, plus about 1¼ cups for coating the cookies
2	teaspoons pure vanilla extract
¼	teaspoon salt
2¼	cups all-purpose flour
¾	cup finely chopped pecans

USING an electric mixer, beat the butter in a large bowl until creamy. Add ½ cup of the confectioners' sugar and beat until smooth. Beat in the vanilla and salt. With the beaters on low speed, mix in the flour just until incorporated. Mix in the pecans. Using your hands, gather the dough into a ball inside the bowl, cover the bowl with plastic wrap, and refrigerate for about 30 minutes. (The dough becomes very firm when refrigerated for a longer time, but it will soften after about 1 hour at room temperature.)

PREHEAT the oven to 375°F. Line 1 or 2 cookie sheets with parchment paper.

PINCH off small clumps of dough and roll into 1-inch balls, arranging them about 1½ inches apart on the prepared sheet(s). Bake for 11 to 12 minutes or until the cookies are lightly golden on the bottom and just barely beginning to color on top. (If using 2 cookie sheets, rotate them from top to bottom and front to back about halfway through baking.) Let the cookies cool on the sheets for about 5 minutes.

PLACE the remaining 1¼ cups of confectioners' sugar in a shallow bowl. While the cookies are still warm, roll them in the sugar to coat. (Be gentle, because the cookies are fragile.) Set them on a rack to cool. Just before serving or storing, recoat the cookies with sugar.

STORE, layered between sheets of wax paper, in an airtight container for up to 2 weeks; or freeze for up to 2 months.

Hazelnut Biscotti

MAKES ABOUT 34 BISCOTTI

Traditional Italian biscotti (the name means "twice cooked") contain eggs, but no butter or oil. The result is a superior crunch that's dry and crisp compared with the more cookie-like American versions, which include butter. These are great for dunking—in coffee, hot chocolate, or sweet dessert wine.

1	cup hazelnuts (see Note)
3	large eggs
1	cup sugar
1	teaspoon baking powder
¼	teaspoon salt
½	teaspoon hazelnut flavoring
2	cups all-purpose flour

PREHEAT the oven to 350°F. Line a large cookie or baking sheet with parchment paper.

PLACE the hazelnuts in a single layer on a small baking sheet. Bake for about 8 minutes or until golden. Spill the nuts into a dish towel and rub them with the towel to remove most of their papery skin. Transfer the nuts to a cutting board and when cool enough to handle, chop coarse.

WHISK the eggs in a large bowl. Spoon off 1½ tablespoons of the beaten eggs and reserve for glazing the biscotti. To the remaining eggs in the bowl, whisk in the sugar, baking powder, salt, and hazelnut flavoring. Add the flour and stir with a wooden spoon just until combined. Stir in the hazelnuts.

DIVIDE the dough in half using a rubber spatula and place each half lengthwise onto one side of the prepared sheet. Flour your hands and shape each sticky clump of dough into a rectangular loaf about 12 inches long and 2½ inches wide. Make sure the loaves are at least 3 inches apart on the sheet. Brush the reserved beaten egg over the tops of the loaves.

BAKE for about 35 minutes or until the loaves are golden brown. Transfer the sheet to a rack to cool for 10 minutes. Reduce the oven temperature to 325°F.

PEEL the loaves off the parchment paper and transfer them, one at a time, to a cutting board. Using a serrated knife in a long sawing motion, cut the loaves on a slight diagonal into ½- to ¾-inch-thick slices. Discard the parchment and place the biscotti, cut side down, on the sheet. Bake for 10 minutes. Turn the pieces over to the other cut side and bake for about 5 minutes more. Transfer the biscotti to a rack to cool.

STORE in an airtight container for about 1 month; or freeze for up to 3 months. (You can perk up the biscotti by toasting them in a 350°F oven for about 5 minutes.)

NOTE: If you prefer almonds to hazelnuts, substitute an equal amount of natural or blanched almonds and use pure almond extract instead of hazelnut flavoring.

Tips FOR MAKING HAND-SHAPED COOKIES

- For most of the cookies in this chapter, the dough is simply rolled between your hands into balls, which bake into more perfect circles than if the dough were just dropped onto the baking sheet. Some recipes call for the balls to be pressed into rounds about ½ inch thick, so get out your ruler, measure the first few so you know how thick they should be, and then make the rest roughly the same size. Do the same if the recipe calls for a specific cookie diameter.

- When rolling dough into balls, do it fairly quickly. If overworked, perfectly smooth rounds will end up softening from the warmth of your hands, which will cause them to spread more than intended during baking.

- If the dough becomes too soft to shape, refrigerate it for 15 to 30 minutes or until it's firm enough to work with.

- Even though the dough for hand-shaped cookies is firm enough to roll into balls, some are still destined to spread in the oven. Space the cookies as suggested in each recipe to give them room.

- Biscotti dough tends to be thick and sticky, so flour your hands well before shaping it on the baking sheet.

Cranberry Pistachio Biscotti

MAKES ABOUT *34* BISCOTTI

The fruit and nut combination of dried cranberries and pistachios is often chosen for its Christmas colors. But it's also the duo's complementary flavors and textures—the cranberries add a chewy, sweet-tartness and the pistachios are rich and buttery tasting—that really entice.

3	cups all-purpose flour
2	teaspoons baking powder
¼	teaspoon ground cinnamon
¼	teaspoon salt
8	tablespoons (1 stick) unsalted butter, softened
1	cup granulated sugar
⅓	cup light brown sugar
2	large eggs
1½	teaspoons pure vanilla extract
1	tablespoon finely grated orange zest (from 1 orange)
1¼	cups shelled unsalted pistachios
1	cup dried cranberries

PREHEAT the oven to 350°F. Line a large cookie or baking sheet with parchment paper.

WHISK together the flour, baking powder, cinnamon, and salt in a medium bowl.

USING an electric mixer, beat the butter in a large bowl until creamy. Add the granulated and brown sugars and beat until fully blended. Beat in the eggs, then the vanilla and orange zest. With the beaters on low speed, mix in the flour mixture just until the dough starts to clump together. Mix in the pistachios and cranberries. Using your hands or a rubber spatula, gather the dough into a ball, then divide it in half.

WITH lightly floured hands, place each half of the dough lengthwise on one side of the prepared sheet. Shape the dough into rectangular loaves about 13 inches long and 2½ inches wide. Make sure the loaves are at least 3 inches apart on the sheet.

BAKE for 30 to 35 minutes, rotating the sheet from front to back about halfway through baking, or until the loaves are nicely golden and the tops feel mostly firm when gently pressed. Transfer the sheet to a rack to cool for 10 minutes. Reduce the oven temperature to 325°F.

PEEL the loaves off the parchment paper and transfer them, one at a time, to a cutting board. Using a serrated knife in a long sawing motion, cut the loaves on a slight diagonal into ¾-inch-thick slices. Discard the parchment and place the biscotti, cut side down, on the sheet. Bake for 10 minutes. Turn the biscotti over to the other cut side and bake for about 10 minutes longer or until lightly toasted. Transfer the biscotti to a rack to cool.

STORE in an airtight container for up to 2 weeks; or freeze for up to 2 months. (You can perk up the biscotti by toasting them in a 350°F oven for about 5 minutes.)

Orange Poppy Seed Drops

MAKES ABOUT 55 COOKIES

These tender rounds have the fresh, citrusy flavor of orange and the crunch of poppy seeds. Their small size makes them rather addictive, as does the pinch of orange sugar on top. Store poppy seeds in the freezer, because they go rancid if left too long at room temperature.

2	cups all-purpose flour
3	tablespoons poppy seeds
¼	teaspoon salt
16	tablespoons (2 sticks) unsalted butter, softened
½	cup sugar, plus ⅓ cup for making the orange sugar
2	large egg yolks
1	teaspoon pure vanilla extract
2	teaspoons finely grated orange zest, plus 1½ teaspoons for making the orange sugar (from about 1 large orange)

PREHEAT the oven to 350°F. Line 2 cookie sheets with parchment paper.

WHISK together the flour, poppy seeds, and salt in a medium bowl.

USING an electric mixer, beat the butter and ½ cup of the sugar in a large bowl until creamy. Beat in the egg yolks. Mix in the vanilla and 2 teaspoons of the orange zest. With the beaters on low speed, mix in the flour mixture just until the dough starts to come together. Using your hands, work the dough into a ball.

TO MAKE the orange sugar: Whisk the remaining ⅓ cup of sugar and 1½ teaspoons of orange zest in a small bowl.

PINCH off small clumps of dough and roll into balls between ¾ and 1 inch in diameter. Place on the prepared sheets, arranging them about 1½ inches apart. Press down on the balls with your fingers to form rounds that are a scant ½ inch thick. Spoon about ¼ teaspoon of orange sugar onto the top of each round, pressing down gently so the sugar adheres.

BAKE for about 13 minutes, rotating the sheets from top to bottom and front to back halfway through baking, or until the edges are golden and the tops feel mostly firm. Transfer the cookies to a rack to cool completely.

STORE, layered between sheets of wax paper, in an airtight container for up to 10 days.

See photograph of Orange Poppy Seed Drops on page 21.

Molasses Ginger Cookies

Stale spices will yield a flat-tasting cookie, so make sure your spices aren't too old. When you open up the jar of ground ginger it should really smell like ginger! Ditto for cinnamon. And no amount of pre-ground nutmeg will beat the flavor of freshly grated.

If you bake these cookies for the time suggested, they will be slightly chewy in the center and crisp around the edge. If you prefer them crunchy all over, bake for about 2 minutes longer.

2	cups all-purpose flour
1	teaspoon baking soda
½	teaspoon salt
2	teaspoons ground ginger
1	teaspoon ground cinnamon
¼	teaspoon ground allspice
¼	teaspoon freshly grated nutmeg
12	tablespoons (1½ sticks) unsalted butter, softened
¾	cup granulated sugar, plus ¼ cup for rolling the dough in
¼	cup packed dark brown sugar
¼	cup molasses
1	large egg

PREHEAT the oven to 350°F. Line 1 or 2 cookie sheets with parchment paper.

WHISK together the flour, baking soda, salt, ginger, cinnamon, allspice, and nutmeg in a medium bowl.

USING an electric mixer, beat the butter in a large bowl until creamy. Add ¾ cup of the granulated sugar and the brown sugar and beat until fully blended. Beat in the molasses, then the egg. With the beaters on low speed, mix in the flour mixture until fully incorporated. The dough will be soft.

PLACE the remaining ¼ cup of granulated sugar in a shallow bowl. Pinch off clumps of dough and roll into 1-inch balls. Roll each ball in the sugar to coat fully. Place the balls about 2 inches apart on the prepared sheet(s). Bake for 11 to 12 minutes or until the cookies still appear soft, even a little wet-looking in the center. (If using 2 sheets, rotate them from top to bottom and front to back about halfway through baking.) Let the cookies cool on the sheet for 2 minutes, then transfer to a rack to cool.

STORE in an airtight container for up to 1 week; or freeze for up to 2 months.

Chocolate Crinkles

MAKES ABOUT 55 COOKIES

The dough is easy, but the waiting is hard. Yes, this dough, which is more like a thick, creamy batter, really requires a thorough chilling that is best accomplished overnight. It needs to be firm enough to roll into balls and cold going into the oven in order to puff and crack as intended. Don't overcook these treasures—they should be tender and fudgy.

8	tablespoons (1 stick) unsalted butter
4	ounces unsweetened chocolate, coarsely chopped
2	cups all-purpose flour
2	teaspoons baking powder
¼	teaspoon salt
3	large eggs
1	cup granulated sugar
¾	cup lightly packed dark brown sugar
1	teaspoon pure vanilla extract
1	cup confectioners' sugar, for coating the dough

MELT the butter and chocolate in a medium, heavy saucepan set over very low heat. Stir constantly until almost fully melted. Remove the pan from the heat and stir until the chocolate is completely melted and smooth.

WHISK together the flour, baking powder, and salt in a medium bowl.

USING an electric mixer, beat the eggs in a large bowl until frothy, about 45 seconds. Add the granulated and brown sugars and beat until thick and smooth, about 1 minute. Beat in the melted chocolate mixture and the vanilla. With the beaters on low speed, mix in the flour mixture just until completely blended. Cover the bowl with plastic wrap and refrigerate until the dough is firm, at least 4 hours but preferably overnight.

PREHEAT the oven to 350°F. Line 1 or 2 cookie sheets with parchment paper.

PLACE the confectioners' sugar in a medium bowl. Set a sheet of wax paper on the work surface in front of you. Using a small spoon, scoop chunks of dough and roll them between your hands into 1-inch balls. Place the balls on the wax paper, forming enough for 1 cookie sheet. (There's no getting around messy, sticky hands; just wash them after each batch.) Drop about 5 balls at a time into the confectioners' sugar and shake the bowl to fully and generously coat them. Arrange them about 2 inches apart on the prepared sheet(s).

BAKE for 11 to 12 minutes or until the cookies are puffed and crackled on top. The tops should be soft, even a little wet-looking, but the edges should feel mostly firm. (If using 2 cookie sheets, rotate them from top to bottom and front to back about halfway through baking.) Slide the parchment off the cookie sheet(s) and onto a wire rack. After a few minutes, remove the cookies from the paper using a thin metal spatula and place them directly onto racks to cool.

STORE, layered between sheets of wax paper, in an airtight container for up to 4 days; or freeze for up to 2 months.

Chocolate Peppermint Cookies

MAKES ABOUT *34* COOKIES

These chocolate rounds topped with peppermint glaze and crushed candy canes make a festive addition to the Christmas dessert table. To crush the candy, place it in a heavy-duty plastic bag and smack it with the smooth side of a meat mallet or hammer. Crush the candy into different size bits, not powder. Sharp edges may prick holes in the bag, so be on the lookout for tiny shards of candy on your countertop.

2   cups all-purpose flour
⅔   cup Dutch-processed cocoa powder
½   teaspoon baking powder
¼   teaspoon salt
12   tablespoons (1½ sticks) unsalted butter, softened
1   cup sugar
1   large egg
1   tablespoon milk
½   teaspoon pure vanilla extract

PEPPERMINT ICING
1½   cups confectioners' sugar
2 to 2½ tablespoons water
¼   teaspoon peppermint flavoring

Garnish: 4 ounces striped candy canes or hard peppermint candies, crushed into bits (about ⅔ cup)

WHISK together the flour, cocoa, baking powder, and salt in a medium bowl.

USING an electric mixer, beat the butter and sugar in a large bowl until creamy. Beat in the egg. Beat in the milk and vanilla. With the beaters on low speed, mix in the flour mixture just until blended and the dough starts to clump together. Gather the dough into a ball, cover with plastic wrap, and refrigerate for at least 1 hour.

PREHEAT the oven to 350°F. Line 2 cookie sheets with parchment paper.

PINCH off small clumps of dough and shape into 1-inch balls, arranging them about 2 inches apart on the prepared sheets. With the heel of your hand, flatten the balls to a scant ½-inch thickness. (The edges may crack in areas, which you can press together, if desired.) Bake for 13 to 14 minutes, rotating the sheets from top to bottom and front to back halfway through baking. The cookies will feel a little soft on top, but they will firm up as they cool. Transfer to a rack to cool completely.

FOR THE PEPPERMINT ICING: Whisk the confectioners' sugar and 2 tablespoons of water in a medium bowl until smooth. Whisk in the peppermint flavoring. The icing should be thick but spreadable. Add a little more water as needed to thin; or add more sugar to thicken.

TO ASSEMBLE the cookies: Place the crushed candy on a plate. Using a frosting spreader or a table knife, glaze the tops of the cookies with icing. Sprinkle some candy over the wet icing, pressing down gently so it adheres. Alternatively, press the cookies icing side down into the candy. Place the cookies on a rack until the icing sets completely.

STORE, layered between sheets of wax paper, in an airtight container for up to 5 days. The cookies look and taste their finest, however, within 2 days of being made. You can freeze the undecorated chocolate rounds for up to 1 month.

Swedish Dreams

MAKES ABOUT *40* COOKIES

My mother's Swedish friend Ulla Lundholm Beauchamp sent me this recipe. Her grandmother would bake these cookies, which in Sweden are called *drommar*, meaning "dreams," every Christmas as well as for other special occasions. What makes them dreamy—and unusual—is their sandy, melt-in-the-mouth texture.

The first step of browning the butter gives the cookies a rich, nutty flavor. The technique can be a little tricky, though, because melted butter goes from caramel-colored to burnt with bitter, blackened specks in seconds if you're not careful. Use moderate heat, as directed, to slowly brown the butter. Heat too high risks burning the butter, while heat that is too low won't allow the butter to brown properly.

16	tablespoons (2 sticks) unsalted butter
¾	cup sugar
2	teaspoons pure vanilla extract
2	cups all-purpose flour
1	teaspoon baking powder
	About 40 whole blanched almonds

HAVE ready a large bowl filled with ice and a second large bowl for pouring the browned butter into when it's done.

MELT the butter in a heavy, medium saucepan over moderate heat. Once melted, the butter will start to foam and bubble. Swirl the pan occasionally and after a total of 6 to 8 minutes—don't take your eyes off the pan!—the butter will turn caramel-colored and smell nutty, and there will be brown specks at the bottom of the pan. Immediately pull the pan from the heat and pour the butter, along with all the brown bits, into the large empty bowl. Set this bowl inside the bowl with the ice and cool the butter until it comes to room temperature and is mostly congealed but still soft. (This should take between 30 and 50 minutes.)

PREHEAT the oven to 325°F. Line a cookie sheet with parchment paper.

REMOVE the bowl of butter from its ice bath. Add the sugar and, using an electric mixer, beat the butter and sugar until white and fluffy, about 1 minute. (There will be dark specks from the browned butter.) Beat in the vanilla. With the beaters on low speed, mix in the flour and baking powder until thoroughly combined. The dough will be soft and crumbly. Using your hands, gather the dough into a ball.

PINCH off small pieces of dough and roll into 1-inch balls, arranging them about 1½ inches apart on the prepared sheet. Gently press an almond onto the center of each cookie. Bake for about 22 minutes or until the cookies are golden. They will feel a little sandy on the outside. Carefully transfer them to a rack to cool.

STORE in an airtight container for up to 2 weeks; or freeze for up to 2 months.

Viennese Crescents

Buttery almond cookies in the shape of crescents are traditional Christmastime treats in Austria. They're known as *Vanillekipferl* for the vanilla sugar that is used in the dough and as a delectable coating.

1¼	cups (about 6½ ounces) whole blanched almonds
½	cup Vanilla Sugar (recipe follows), plus another ½ cup for coating the cookies
16	tablespoons (2 sticks) unsalted butter, softened
2¼	cups all-purpose flour
¼	teaspoon salt

COMBINE the almonds and ½ cup of vanilla sugar in a food processor. Process until the nuts are finely ground.

USING an electric mixer, beat the butter in a large bowl until creamy. Add the ground almond–sugar mixture and beat until well blended. With the beaters on low speed, mix in the flour and salt just until thoroughly combined. Using your hands, work the dough into a ball. Wrap the dough in plastic wrap and refrigerate for 1 hour or until firm. (If refrigerated for a longer time, the dough will become very hard, so just let it sit at room temperature for about one hour to soften before shaping.)

PREHEAT the oven to 350°F. Line 1 or 2 cookie sheets with parchment paper.

BREAK off clumps of dough a little larger than 1 inch in diameter and squeeze or roll them into little logs about 2½ inches long. Place them on the prepared sheet(s) and, with your fingers, shape the dough into crescents with tapered ends. Arrange them about 2 inches apart on the prepared sheet(s).

BAKE the cookies for about 15 minutes or until light golden. (If using 2 cookie sheets, rotate them from top to bottom and front to back halfway through baking.) Let the cookies sit on the sheets for about 2 minutes, then carefully transfer them to a rack.

PLACE the remaining ½ cup vanilla sugar in a shallow bowl. While the crescents are still warm, gently roll them in the sugar to coat. (Handle the cookies carefully because they're fragile.) Set them on a wire rack to cool completely.

STORE, layered between sheets of wax paper, in an airtight container for up to 10 days; or freeze for up to 2 months.

Vanilla Sugar

You can make vanilla sugar two different ways depending on how much time you have. (1) For immediate use, combine 2 cups of granulated sugar and ½ to 1 vanilla bean, cut into ¾-inch lengths, in a food processor. Process until only tiny bits of the bean are visible, 1 to 2 minutes. (Pick out and discard any bits larger than the size of chocolate sprinkles.) Store leftover vanilla sugar in a covered jar. (2) When making ahead, bury 1 vanilla bean in about 2 cups of granulated sugar in a large jar. Cover, shake a few times, and let stand for 1 week or up to 1 year. The bean will perfume the sugar over time. As you use the vanilla sugar, add more plain sugar to the jar.

Peanut Butter Chocolate Kisses

MAKES ABOUT 48 COOKIES

These treats, which are also called peanut blossoms, are great fun to make with children. Let the kids help assemble the dough and roll it into balls. But the really fun part comes when it's time to press chocolate kisses into the just-baked cookies. Two words of caution: Watch out for small hands near the hot baking sheets, and make sure to have more than enough kisses because some will magically disappear as you're baking.

1⅔ cups all-purpose flour
1 teaspoon baking soda
½ teaspoon salt
8 tablespoons (1 stick) unsalted butter, softened
¾ cup creamy peanut butter
1 cup lightly packed dark brown sugar
1 large egg
1 teaspoon pure vanilla extract
About ⅓ cup granulated sugar, for coating the balls
About 48 Hershey's Kisses, unwrapped

Tip: Spraying the inside of a glass measuring cup with non-stick baking spray will make it easier to scrape out the peanut butter after measuring it.

PREHEAT the oven to 375°F. Line 2 cookie sheets with parchment paper.

WHISK together the flour, baking soda, and salt in a medium bowl.

USING an electric mixer, beat the butter in a large bowl until creamy. Beat in the peanut butter, then the brown sugar. Add the egg and vanilla and beat until blended. With the beaters on low speed, mix in the flour mixture until fully combined.

PLACE the granulated sugar in a medium bowl. Roll the dough into 1-inch balls, and then roll each ball in sugar to coat completely. Place the balls on the prepared sheets, arranging them about 1½ inches apart. Bake for 10 minutes, rotating the sheets from top to bottom and front to back about halfway through baking, or until the cookies are puffed and cracked on top. (The cookies will be soft, but they will firm up as they cool.) Remove the sheets from the oven and immediately press a chocolate kiss into the center of each hot cookie. Transfer the cookies to a rack to cool completely.

STORE in an airtight container for up to 5 days.

Italian Wine Cookies

MAKES ABOUT *36* COOKIES

At a Christmas cookie swap I attended a few years ago, these unusual S-shaped cookies caught my eye. Maybe it was the cinnamon sugar coating or maybe it was because they looked crunchy. After the baker, Lena Giordano of Waltham, Massachusetts, finished describing the treats she had brought, I pounced. It was love at first crunch. And within two hours of my receiving the recipe in the mail, the ingredients were in my mixing bowl. Truth be told, there's not an easier dough in this book to assemble nor one that's as much fun to shape with your hands. To top it off, these treats are low in saturated fat, as they contain no butter or eggs.

Lena's cookies contain aniseed, which are tiny, greenish-gray, licorice-flavored seeds. Their subtle flavor makes these not-too-sweet biscuits particularly suited to serving after dinner with wine. If this spice doesn't appeal, you can omit the seeds.

2	cups all-purpose flour
½	cup sugar
2	teaspoons baking powder
¼	teaspoon salt
1½	tablespoons aniseed (also called anise seed)
½	cup white wine
½	cup olive oil

CINNAMON SUGAR

6	tablespoons sugar
2	tablespoons ground cinnamon

PREHEAT the oven to 350°F. Line 1 or 2 cookie sheets with parchment paper.

WHISK together the flour, sugar, baking powder, salt, and aniseed in a large bowl. Using a wooden spoon, stir in the wine and olive oil until fully combined.

FOR THE CINNAMON SUGAR: Whisk together the sugar and cinnamon in a shallow bowl.

PINCH off 1-inch chunks of dough and roll them between your hands (or on a flat surface) to form thin ropes about 6 inches long and about the thickness of a pencil. Gently toss in the cinnamon sugar to coat. Shape the ropes into an S and place on the prepared sheet(s), arranging them about 1½ inches apart. Bake for 17 to 20 minutes or until the cookies are browned and feel mostly firm. (They will firm up more as they cool; the longer time yields a crunchier and slightly darker cookie.) If using 2 cookie sheets, rotate them from top to bottom and front to back about halfway through baking. Transfer the cookies to a rack to cool.

STORE in an airtight container for up to 2 weeks.

Tip: Save your more expensive and peppery olive oils for salads and use a mild-flavored variety for these cookies.

Filled and Sandwich Cookies

Tips FOR MAKING FILLED AND SANDWICH COOKIES

Filled and sandwich cookies are a little more time-consuming than other treats. Preparing the filling (unless it's just fruit preserves) adds an additional step; and for sandwich cookies, the recipe yield is cut in half, since it takes two to make a sandwich. But don't let this stop you! These cookies are special and they look charming. Because they're a little out of the ordinary, these treats are much appreciated at holiday time.

- Three of the cookies in this chapter—Baby Butter and Jam Sandwiches, Fig Half-Moons, and the Linzer Cookies—are made from dough that is rolled out, so refer to the tips for rolled cookies on page 42.

- When filling cookies, a little less is usually better than more. Too much fig paste in the Fig Half-Moons will cause it to seep through the seams while baking. Too much jam in the Baby Butter and Jam Sandwiches or Linzer Cookies and it will dribble out when the treats are bitten into.

- After the cookies are sandwiched around a filling they will start to soften. Unless you prefer them that way, it's best to store the rounds unfilled and then assemble the cookies close to serving time.

Baby Butter and Jam Sandwiches

MAKES ABOUT 36 SANDWICH COOKIES

These cookies are incredibly cute. In fact, they're downright adorable. Not only will young and old cookie fans find these tender, buttery wafers sandwiching a layer of jam irresistible, but everyone will think you went to much more trouble than you did.

10 tablespoons (1 1/4 sticks) unsalted butter, softened
1/2 cup confectioners' sugar, plus more for dusting the cookies
1 1/2 cups all-purpose flour
1/4 teaspoon salt
Raspberry preserves (or strawberry or apricot preserves or some of each)

Tip: The first time I made these I couldn't find my 1 1/2-inch round cookie cutter. I ended up using one of those little plastic cups that come with a bottle of cough syrup. The rim was a perfect 1 1/2 inches! And the cup can be gently squeezed to loosen any cutouts that get stuck.

COOKIE CUTTER NEEDED: 1 1/2-inch round

USING an electric mixer, beat the butter in a large bowl until creamy. Beat in the 1/2 cup of confectioners' sugar until fully blended. With the beaters on low speed, mix in the flour and salt until thoroughly combined. Using your hands, gather the dough into a ball, then press it into a disk and wrap in plastic wrap. Refrigerate for about 1 hour or until the dough is firm enough to roll out. (If refrigerated longer, let the dough sit at room temperature for 30 to 45 minutes to soften before rolling.)

PREHEAT the oven to 325°F. Line 2 cookie sheets with parchment paper.

ROLL out the dough on a lightly floured surface to a thickness of between 1/8 and 1/4 inch. Using the cutter, stamp out circles close together and arrange them about 1 1/2 inches apart on the prepared sheets. Reroll the scraps two or three times. (Working the dough too much can make it tough.)

BAKE for 10 to 12 minutes, rotating the sheets from top to bottom and front to back about halfway through baking, or until the cookies are just beginning to color and the edges are pale golden. Transfer the cookies to a rack to cool completely.

TO ASSEMBLE: Spread a little of the preserves on the bottom side of half of the rounds, taking care not to spread it too close to the edge. Top with another round, right side up. Just before serving, sift confectioners' sugar over the sandwich cookies.

STORE the plain rounds in an airtight container for up to 1 week. Once the cookies are spread with jam, they'll start to soften after 1 to 2 days.

Chocolate Almond Macaroon Sandwiches

MAKES ABOUT *30* SANDWICH COOKIES

These crisp-chewy macaroons sandwiched around a layer of creamy chocolate ganache are a chocolate lover's dream. You can even turn the treats into a triple threat by drizzling melted dark or white chocolate over the tops of the cookie sandwiches.

4	ounces slivered or whole blanched almonds
2	cups confectioners' sugar
¼	cup Dutch-processed cocoa powder
4	large egg whites
	Pinch of salt
2	tablespoons granulated sugar

CHOCOLATE GANACHE

4	ounces fine-quality bittersweet chocolate, chopped
⅔	cup heavy cream

PREHEAT the oven to 400°F. Line a cookie sheet with parchment paper.

PROCESS the almonds in a food processor until finely ground. (You should have about 1 cup ground almonds.) Add the confectioners' sugar and cocoa and pulse a few times until blended.

USING an electric mixer, beat the egg whites with the salt in a large, clean bowl until they hold soft peaks. Add the granulated sugar and beat until the whites hold stiff peaks. Using a firm rubber spatula, fold in the almond mixture. Make sure no streaks of whites or clumps of almonds remain.

DROP the batter by scant tablespoonfuls onto the prepared sheet using a small spoon or a finger of your free hand to push the batter off the spoon. Form rounds that are about 1¼ to 1½ inches in diameter, arranged about 2 inches apart. (Alternatively, you can use a pastry bag to pipe the rounds.) Try to make the cookies the same size or else it will be hard to find partners for sandwiching.

BAKE the macaroons in the middle of the oven for 7 to 8 minutes or until the tops appear dry and slightly crackled but the insides are still soft. Slide the parchment paper off the cookie sheet and onto a rack.

Let the macaroons sit for about 5 minutes. Using a metal spatula, carefully transfer the cookies to a rack to cool completely.

FOR THE CHOCOLATE GANACHE: Place the chocolate in a heat-proof bowl. In a small saucepan, heat the cream just to boiling, then carefully pour it over the chocolate. Using a whisk or rubber spatula, gently stir to melt the chocolate. When the chocolate is melted and the mixture is smooth, refrigerate the ganache until it thickens to spreading consistency, about 30 minutes. (If the chilled ganache becomes too firm, particularly if it's made ahead, place the bowl in a pan of warm water and stir until the ganache softens.)

TO ASSEMBLE: Spread about 1½ teaspoons of ganache on the bottoms of half of the macaroons. Top with another macaroon, right side up. These are best assembled the day you're serving.

STORE the plain macaroons in an airtight container for up to 3 days. Once they're spread with ganache, they'll keep, refrigerated in an airtight container, for a few days but will soften.

Tip: Follow the second shortcut on page 1 and have the next batch of macaroons ready to go on a clean sheet of parchment. Slide the parchment onto the cookie sheet and immediately place in the oven.

Chocolate Caramel Thumbprints

Most thumbprints are butter cookies with an indentation—made with the poke of a thumb, which is how the cookie got its name—that is filled with jam. Although there's nothing wrong with that, I thought a jazzier version for the holidays, something in chocolate, would be more fun to make and scrumptious to eat. Here, the cookie is chocolate, the well is filled with chewy caramel, and a drizzle of dark chocolate tops it off. Jazzy, indeed.

2	cups all-purpose flour
½	cup Dutch-processed cocoa powder
½	teaspoon salt
16	tablespoons (2 sticks) unsalted butter, softened
1¼	cups sugar
1	large egg
1	large egg yolk
1	teaspoon pure vanilla extract

CARAMEL FILLING

20	caramels (about 5½ ounces), such as Kraft candies, unwrapped
¼	cup heavy (or whipping) cream

CHOCOLATE DRIZZLE

4½	ounces bittersweet chocolate, chopped

WHISK together the flour, cocoa, and salt in a medium bowl.

USING an electric mixer, beat the butter in a large bowl until creamy. Add the sugar and beat well until fluffy. Beat in the whole egg and egg yolk. Mix in the vanilla. With the beaters on low speed, mix in the flour mixture until incorporated and the dough comes together. Gather the dough into a ball, then divide it in half. Wrap each half separately in plastic wrap and refrigerate until firm, about 1 hour.

PREHEAT the oven to 350°F. Line 2 cookie sheets with parchment paper.

WORKING with one half of the dough at a time (leave the remainder in the refrigerator), roll it into 1-inch balls, arranging them about 2 inches apart on the prepared sheets. Make an indentation in the center of each ball using the handle end of a wooden spoon (or use your thumb or a knuckle), being careful not to go all the way through the dough.

BAKE for about 13 minutes, rotating the sheets from top to bottom and front to back about halfway through baking, or until the cookies feel just slightly firm. Transfer the cookie sheets to a rack and immediately depress the centers of the cookies again using the handle end of a wooden spoon to reinforce and widen the indentation to about ¾ inch in diameter. Transfer the cookies to a rack to cool completely.

FOR THE CARAMEL FILLING: Heat the caramels and cream in a medium saucepan over moderately low heat, stirring often, until the caramels are melted and the mixture is smooth, about 5 minutes. Using the smallest, pointiest spoon you have, such as a demitasse spoon, spoon the caramel into the indentations in the cookies, filling just up to the rim. If the caramel becomes too thick, place the saucepan back over low heat for a few seconds. Let the caramel set before drizzling the cookies with chocolate.

FOR THE CHOCOLATE DRIZZLE: Melt the chocolate in a microwave-safe bowl in the microwave for 20- to 30-second intervals on medium power, stirring after each interval, until melted and smooth. Let cool at room temperature for a few minutes. Place the cookies close together, but not touching, on racks set over wax paper. Pour the chocolate into a small plastic bag (or squeeze bottle). Seal the bag and make a tiny cut in one corner. Working quickly, drizzle the chocolate in a zigzag pattern over the cookies. Let the chocolate set completely before storing the cookies.

STORE, layered between sheets of wax paper, in an airtight container for up to 4 days; or refrigerate for up to 2 weeks.

Linzer Cookies

MAKES ABOUT *22* SANDWICH COOKIES

The centuries-old Linzertorte from Austria is a tart made from a ground-nut dough, filled with either raspberry preserves or currant jam and recognized by its distinctive lattice top. At some point, an industrious baker turned the famous dessert into a cookie, which I'm thankful for because they're easier to make!

1	cup hazelnuts, toasted and skinned (see page 20), or substitute almonds
¾	cup granulated sugar
2¼	cups all-purpose flour
1	teaspoon ground cinnamon
½	teaspoon baking powder
½	teaspoon salt
13	tablespoons (1 stick plus 5 tablespoons) chilled unsalted butter, cut into small chunks
1	large egg
1	large egg yolk
1	teaspoon pure vanilla extract
1	teaspoon finely grated lemon zest
	Raspberry or blackberry preserves
	Confectioners' sugar, for dusting the cookies

COOKIE CUTTERS NEEDED: one 2½-inch round, preferably with fluted or scalloped edges, and one 1-inch round, with fluted or petal-shaped edges

PLACE the hazelnuts in a food processor and process until finely ground. Add the granulated sugar and process until blended. Add the flour, cinnamon, baking powder, and salt and pulse a few times to combine. Add the butter and process until it's chopped into tiny bits. Add the whole egg, egg yolk, vanilla, and lemon zest and process just until the dough starts to clump together and feels moist when pinched. Turn the dough out onto a clean surface and gather it into a ball. Divide it in half, press each half into a disk, and wrap separately in plastic wrap. Refrigerate the disks for at least 2 hours. (Or freeze for up to 3 months.)

PREHEAT the oven to 325°F. Line 2 cookie sheets with parchment paper.

WORKING with one half of the dough at a time (keep the other disk refrigerated), roll it out on a lightly floured surface to a ³⁄₁₆- to ¼-inch thickness. Using the 2½-inch round cutter, stamp out circles. Transfer half of the circles to the prepared sheets, arranging them about 1½ inches apart. Using the 1-inch cutter, cut out the centers of the remaining circles, forming rings that will be the tops of the cookie sandwiches. Transfer the rings to the prepared sheets. Gather the scraps into a ball and reroll. (Chill the dough if it becomes too soft.)

BAKE for 15 to 16 minutes, rotating the sheets from top to bottom and front to back about halfway through baking, or until the cookies are lightly golden. Transfer the cookies to a rack to cool completely.

TO ASSEMBLE: Spread about 1½ teaspoons of preserves on the top side of the full circles. (Don't spread it all the way to the edge.) Cover with a ring, right side up. Just before serving, lightly sift confectioners' sugar over the cookies.

STORE the assembled cookie sandwiches (without dusting with confectioners' sugar), layered between sheets of wax paper, in an airtight container for up to 2 days. (The cookies will soften slightly.) The plain cookies can be stored in an airtight container for up to 10 days; or freeze for up to 2 months.

See photograph of Linzer Cookies on page 8.

Fig Half-Moons

MAKES ABOUT *46* COOKIES

Fig is a popular filling for pastries and cookies at Christmastime, especially in the Italian tradition. Here, an orange-scented fig paste is tucked into rich pastry dough that is formed into half-moon shapes. A little more work than the average cookie, these treats are well worth it.

FIG FILLING

- 2 cups (about 12 ounces) halved dried Calimyrna (golden) figs, hard tips discarded
- 1 teaspoon grated orange zest
- ½ cup orange juice
- ¼ cup brandy (or water)
- 1½ tablespoons sugar
- ¼ teaspoon ground cinnamon

PASTRY DOUGH

- 2 cups all-purpose flour
- 1½ tablespoons sugar
- ½ teaspoon salt
- 16 tablespoons (2 sticks) chilled unsalted butter, cut into ½-inch slices
- 8 ounces cream cheese, cut into chunks

Egg wash: 1 large egg whisked with 1 teaspoon cold water
Coarse white sugar, for sprinkling on the cookies

COOKIE CUTTER NEEDED: 3-inch round (or use the rim of a glass)

FOR THE FIG FILLING: Combine the figs, orange zest, orange juice, brandy, sugar, and cinnamon in a medium saucepan. Bring the liquid to a boil, then reduce the heat to moderate, cover, and simmer for 5 minutes or until the liquid is reduced by about half and the figs are softened. Remove from the heat and cool (uncovered).

PROCESS the figs and liquid in a food processor until the mixture is a thick paste. (This can be made up to 1 week ahead and refrigerated.)

FOR THE PASTRY DOUGH: Place the flour, sugar, and salt in a food processor. Pulse once to combine. Add the butter and cream cheese and process just until the dough starts to clump together. Pinch the dough: It should feel moist and stick together. If not, pulse a few more times. Turn the dough out onto a sheet of plastic wrap and gather it into a ball. Divide it in half, press each half into a disk, and wrap separately in plastic wrap. Refrigerate for at least 2 hours or overnight.

PREHEAT the oven to 350°F. Line a cookie sheet with parchment paper.

WORKING with one disk at a time, roll out the dough on a floured surface to a ⅛- to 3/16-inch thickness. (The thinner the better, but not so thin that it tears.) Using the cutter, stamp out circles close together. Reroll the scraps.

USING a thin metal spatula, transfer the circles to a sheet of wax paper. Place a rounded teaspoonful of fig paste on one half of each dough circle (at least ¼ inch away from the edge). Using a pastry brush, dab a tiny bit of the egg wash along the edge of the dough in a semicircle around the filling. Fold the half of the circle without the fig filling over the filling to enclose, forming a half-moon shape. Gently press the edges together to seal.

PLACE the half-moons on the prepared cookie sheet, arranging them about 1½ inches apart. Crimp the sealed edges with the tines of a fork. (You can assemble and refrigerate the half-moons up to 1 day ahead; or freeze them on a cookie sheet, then wrap them up in a sturdy plastic bag. Freeze for up to 2 months. Thaw at room temperature for about 1 hour before continuing with the recipe.)

LIGHTLY brush the tops of the half-moons with egg wash and sprinkle liberally with coarse sugar. Bake for 20 to 23 minutes or until nicely golden. For even baking, rotate the cookie sheet from front to back halfway through baking. Transfer the cookies to a rack to cool.

STORE in an airtight container for up to 5 days, but these are best within 2 days of baking. To freshen and recrisp, heat on a baking sheet in a 375°F oven for 3 to 4 minutes.

Bar Cookies

Tips FOR MAKING BAR COOKIES

- With bar cookies you get a big bang for your baking time because all the dough is baked at one time in one pan—no shaping, rolling, or stamping required. The other advantage is that you get to choose how large or small they should be *after* baking. Most of these treats are thick or rich or both, so cutting them into small one- or two-bite-size pieces may work best. If you're baking for a crowd, you'll get more mileage from little squares.

- All kinds of tasty treats can come from a baking pan, including cheesecake and lemon squares, chocolate-covered toffee, peanut brittle bars, and, of course, brownies. Some of the bars in this chapter consist of a crust, made of shortbread dough or pressed-in cookie crumbs, and a rich topping. In these cases, the crust is always baked first. Make sure to spread the dough evenly in the pan so the crust bakes properly; thin spots will brown too fast and thick areas will be underdone. You might think there isn't enough dough for the Toffee Bars or Turtle Bars, but trust me, there is!

- To make cutting and removing the bars from the pan easier, as well as to avoid scratching the pan's surface, some of the recipes call for the pan to be lined with foil. The easiest way to do this is to turn the pan upside down and press

a sheet of foil—cut at least six inches longer than the length of the pan—over it, creasing the foil along the edges and corners of the pan. Flip the pan over and carefully fit the foil inside. The next step is buttering the foil. Don't even think about using a cold-hard chunk of butter because it will dislodge or tear the foil. Instead, use softened butter applied with a pastry brush, a crumpled piece of wax paper, or your fingers. You can also grease the foil with clear, flavorless oil (such as vegetable or canola) or coat it with nonstick baking spray. Greasing the pan *before* lining it with foil helps the foil adhere to the pan.

- Follow the recipe instructions for when to cut the cookies. In some cases, as with the Almond Thins, Chocolate Shortbread Wedges, and Peanut Brittle Bars, the cookies must be cut while still warm; otherwise they harden and become almost impossible to cut neatly. In most other recipes, the bars are cut when thoroughly cooled or after any topping has set.

- You can use a bench scraper, a thin-bladed knife, or a pizza cutter to cut bars. I love the bench scraper for this job because it's inserted straight down, making a clean cut, rather than on an angle and dragged like a knife is. Wiping the scraper or knife clean of crumbs after each cut will yield neater edges.

Apricot Almond Bars

MAKES *24* BARS

A duet of apricot and almond plays sweetly in these rich, buttery bars. You'll find that these treats are a wonderful addition to cookie platters for holiday brunches and festive open houses as well as piled into gift boxes to give to friends and family.

14 tablespoons (1¾ sticks) unsalted butter, softened
½   cup sugar
1¾ cups all-purpose flour
¼   teaspoon salt
3½ ounces (scant ½ cup) almond paste
⅓   cup sliced almonds, plus 2 tablespoons for sprinkling
1   cup apricot preserves

PREHEAT the oven to 350°F. Line a 9-inch square baking pan with foil so that it extends about 2 inches over two opposite sides. Generously butter the foil, making sure the sides and the bottom are well coated to prevent the bars from sticking.

USING an electric mixer, beat the butter and sugar in a large bowl until creamy. With the beaters on low speed, mix in the flour and salt just until blended. The dough will be crumbly, but it will feel moist when pinched. Scoop out 1 cup of the dough and set it aside in a small bowl. Press the remaining dough evenly in the prepared pan. (Flour your fingers if the dough sticks to them.) Bake the crust for 23 to 25 minutes or until golden. Cool for 5 minutes.

MEANWHILE, crumble the almond paste into small bits and toss with the reserved dough in the bowl. Mix in ⅓ cup of the almonds.

SPREAD the apricot preserves over the baked crust. Sprinkle the almond paste–crumb topping evenly over the preserves. Sprinkle with the remaining 2 tablespoons of almonds. Bake for 32 to 35 minutes or until the preserves are bubbling and the topping is nicely golden. (Take a whiff when the bars come out of the oven . . . they are incredibly fragrant!) Cool completely in the pan on a rack.

HOLDING on to the foil overhang, lift the bars from the pan and place on a cutting board. Peel the foil away from the sides of the bars, using a knife to remove the foil, if necessary. Using a sharp knife or a bench scraper, cut into 4 equal strips, then cut each strip crosswise into 6 bars.

STORE, layered between sheets of wax paper, in an airtight container for up to 4 days; or refrigerate for up to 2 weeks; or freeze for up to 2 months.

Baci Brownies

Touring around Italy many years ago, I figured that a few miles of daily walking warranted two gelatos a day. One of those was always the flavor called *baci*. Not only did *baci* sound romantic (it means "kisses"), but the gelato paired the chocolate and hazelnut that I loved so much in the rich little candies of the same name. These fudgy brownies with a swirl of Nutella, the hazelnut-cocoa spread from Italy, plus a sprinkling of toasted hazelnuts will have everyone wanting to kiss the cook.

1	cup (about 4½ ounces) hazelnuts
1	cup all-purpose flour
½	teaspoon baking powder
½	teaspoon salt
12	tablespoons (1½ sticks) unsalted butter
6	ounces unsweetened chocolate, coarsely chopped
2	cups sugar
3	large eggs
1½	teaspoons pure vanilla extract

NUTELLA SWIRL

½	cup Nutella
1	large egg
1	tablespoon all-purpose flour

PREHEAT the oven to 325°F. Line a 9 × 13-inch baking pan with foil, making sure there's at least a 2-inch overhang on both of the short sides. Gently press the foil into the corners. Butter the foil.

PLACE the hazelnuts on a small baking sheet and toast in the oven for 8 to 10 minutes, stirring once or twice, until lightly golden. Spill the nuts onto a dish towel and rub them with the towel to loosen and remove most of the skin. Transfer the nuts to a cutting board and chop coarse.

WHISK together the flour, baking powder, and salt in a small bowl.

MELT the butter and chocolate in a large saucepan over very low heat, stirring often, until smooth. Remove from the heat and whisk in the sugar. Add the eggs one at a time, whisking after each addition. Mix in the vanilla. Using a rubber spatula, stir in the flour mixture until fully incorporated, then stir in one-third of the toasted hazelnuts. Spread the batter in the prepared pan.

FOR THE NUTELLA SWIRL: Combine the Nutella, egg, and flour in a glass measuring cup and stir with a fork until thoroughly blended. Drop small spoonfuls of the Nutella mixture evenly over the brownie batter. Use a knife to gently swirl it through the batter.

Brownie Slicing Tip:

Brownie Slicing Tip:
A thin-bladed knife dipped in hot water and then dried will make slicing the brownies easier. Wipe the knife clean of sticky, fudgy crumbs after each slice.

SPRINKLE the remaining hazelnuts on top. Bake in the middle of the oven for 35 to 38 minutes or until the top is set and the edges have begun to pull away from the sides of the pan. Don't overbake or the edges will be dry. Cool in the pan on a rack for at least 2 hours.

HOLDING on to the two foil ends, lift the brownie up and onto a cutting board. Peel the foil away from the sides of the brownie. Cut lengthwise into quarters, then cut crosswise into 8 strips to yield 32 bars. Because these are so rich, you can also cut them into 10 or 12 strips to make 40 or 48 smaller bars, respectively.

STORE, layered between sheets of wax paper, in an airtight container for up to 4 days; or refrigerate, tightly wrapped, for up to 1 week; or freeze for up to 2 months.

Cranberry Swirl Cheesecake Squares

MAKES *16* SQUARES

Cheesecake you can eat with your fingers is a real boon at holiday parties. This variety comes on a graham cracker crust and has a swirl of cranberry sauce running through it. The cranberry sauce takes just minutes to prepare, but if you're pressed for time you can substitute ½ cup canned cranberry sauce or ⅓ cup raspberry or strawberry jam.

CRANBERRY SAUCE

- 1 cup fresh or frozen cranberries
- ⅓ cup sugar

CRUST

- 16 graham cracker squares (8 full rectangles)
- 5 tablespoons plus 1 teaspoon (⅓ cup) unsalted butter
- 1 tablespoon light brown sugar

TOPPING

- 8 ounces cream cheese, softened
- ¼ cup sugar
- 1 large egg
- 2 tablespoons milk
- 1 tablespoon fresh lemon juice
- 1 teaspoon pure vanilla extract

FOR THE CRANBERRY SAUCE: Combine the cranberries, sugar, and 2 tablespoons of water in a small saucepan and heat over medium-high heat. Stir to dissolve the sugar. Bring to a boil, then reduce the heat to medium and simmer, stirring occasionally, for about 5 minutes or until the berries have popped and the liquid has been reduced to a thick, syrupy glaze. Transfer the cranberry sauce to a small container (there will be about ½ cup) and refrigerate until needed.

FOR THE CRUST: Preheat the oven to 350°F. Line an 8-inch square baking pan with foil, leaving at least 2 inches hanging over two opposite sides. Butter the foil.

PLACE the graham crackers in a sturdy plastic bag and crush them with the smooth side of a meat mallet until the crumbs are fine. (Alternatively, grind the crackers in a food processor.) You should have about 1½ cups of crumbs.

MELT the butter in a medium saucepan over low heat. Remove from the heat and stir in the brown sugar, then mix in the graham cracker crumbs until fully moistened. Scoop out ½ cup of the crumb mixture and reserve. Press the remaining crumbs evenly in the prepared pan. Bake for 10 minutes. Let cool on a rack for at least 5 minutes. (Maintain the oven temperature.)

FOR THE TOPPING: Using an electric mixer, beat the cream cheese and sugar in a large bowl until smooth. Add the egg, milk, lemon juice, and vanilla and beat to blend well. Pour the mixture over the crust.

USING a small spoon, drop the cranberry sauce onto the cream cheese mixture, making four equally spaced stripes (like narrow rivers of sauce). Give the pan a quarter turn and run the spoon crosswise, wiggling it slightly, through the cranberry stripes every inch or so to create a marbling effect. Sprinkle the reserved ½ cup of crumbs over the top.

BAKE in the middle of the oven for about 30 minutes or until the cheesecake is set. (The tip of a knife inserted into the center will come out mostly clean and will leave a mark.) Transfer the pan to a rack to cool completely.

HOLDING on to the foil overhang, lift the cheesecake and place it on a cutting board. Carefully peel away the foil from the sides. Cut into 16 squares. Serve at room temperature or chilled.

STORE, layered between sheets of wax paper, in an airtight container in the refrigerator for up to 4 days.

Almond Thins

I'm a crunch lover and my son Alex likes soft-chewy sweets. When it comes to these thin, almond-sprinkled bars, we couldn't agree more! He prefers the slightly softer, chewier bars from the center of the pan and I, of course, reach for the crisp edges. Who says you can't satisfy all of the people all of the time?

16	tablespoons (2 sticks) unsalted butter, softened
1	cup sugar, plus 1 tablespoon for sprinkling on top
1	large egg, separated
1	teaspoon pure vanilla extract
½	teaspoon pure almond extract
2	cups all-purpose flour
¼	teaspoon salt
1	cup sliced almonds

PREHEAT the oven to 350°F. Generously butter (including up the sides) a 10½ × 15½ × 1-inch jelly roll pan.

USING an electric mixer, beat the butter in a large bowl until creamy. Add 1 cup of the sugar and beat well for 1 minute until fluffy. Beat in the egg yolk, then the vanilla and almond extracts until thoroughly combined. With the beaters on low speed, mix in the flour and salt until incorporated and the dough just starts to clump together.

DROP the dough, in clumps, into the prepared pan. Using the heel of your hand or lightly floured fingertips, press the dough in evenly. (Thin spots will brown faster so spread it as evenly as possible.)

WHISK the egg white in a small bowl until frothy. Using a pastry brush, brush it all over the dough. Sprinkle with the almonds, pressing them in gently. Sprinkle with the remaining tablespoon of sugar.

BAKE in the middle of the oven for 23 to 25 minutes or until golden brown all over. (If your jelly roll pan is insulated, it will probably take the longer time or slightly more.) Let the pan cool on a rack for 10 minutes. While still warm, cut into quarters lengthwise, then cut crosswise into 10 strips to yield 40 bars. When they are firm enough to remove from the pan without crumbling, use a thin metal spatula to transfer them to a rack to cool.

STORE, layered between sheets of wax paper, in an airtight container for up to 10 days; or freeze for up to 2 months.

Peanut Brittle Bars

MAKES *16* SQUARES

After I learned how to make peanut brittle in my middle school home economics class, it became one of my favorite holiday pursuits. How wrong could I go with only sugar and peanuts? These bars, made with just a few more ingredients, have a similar sweet-salty, toffee-like taste and hard-crunchy texture. The recipe was inspired by dessert doyenne Maida Heatter, whose books I've enjoyed baking from for years.

8	tablespoons (1 stick) unsalted butter, softened
1/4	cup granulated sugar
1/4	cup light brown sugar
1/2	teaspoon pure vanilla extract
1	cup all-purpose flour
1/2	cup salted peanuts, coarsely chopped

PREHEAT the oven to 375°F. Have ready an ungreased 8-inch square baking pan.

USING an electric mixer, beat the butter in a large bowl until creamy. Add the granulated and brown sugars and beat until fully blended. Mix in the vanilla. With the beaters on low speed, mix in the flour, then mix in the peanuts. Transfer the dough to the pan, pressing it in evenly with your fingers to make a firm, smooth layer.

BAKE for 22 to 24 minutes or until golden brown. Cool in the pan for 5 to 10 minutes. While still warm, cut into 16 squares. (Warning: These will be too hard to cut if you let them cool completely.) Cool for about 10 minutes more in the pan and then remove the bars using a narrow metal spatula. Place on a rack to finish cooling.

STORE in an airtight container for up to 2 weeks; or freeze for up to 3 months.

Chocolate Shortbread Wedges

MAKES *16* WEDGES

Oh, so rich, buttery, and chocolaty . . . this is a sophisticated treat for chocolate lovers. Serve the shortbread with a pot of your finest coffee.

1½ cups all-purpose flour

¼ cup Dutch-processed cocoa powder

¼ teaspoon salt

12 tablespoons (1½ sticks) unsalted butter, softened

½ cup sugar

1 teaspoon pure vanilla extract

LIGHTLY butter a 9½-inch fluted tart pan with a removable bottom.

WHISK together the flour, cocoa, and salt in a medium bowl.

USING an electric mixer, beat the butter in a large bowl until creamy. Add the sugar and beat well until fully blended. Mix in the vanilla. With the beaters on low speed, mix in the flour mixture until fully incorporated. (At first the dough will resemble fine crumbs, but after a little more beating the dough will come together in soft clumps.) Spread the dough in the prepared pan, pressing it in evenly with your fingers to flatten and smooth the top. Refrigerate for at least 1 hour or until firm.

PREHEAT the oven to 300°F. Prick the dough with a fork every inch or so (going all the way through to the pan bottom) in 2 concentric circles. Press around the rim with the tines of the fork to make small decorative lines. Bake in the upper middle of the oven for 63 to 65 minutes or until the shortbread feels mostly firm around the edge and semifirm in the center. Cool on a rack for 10 minutes.

CAREFULLY remove the outer ring of the tart pan. (I do this by setting the pan on a small bowl and letting the ring drop down.) Place the shortbread, still on the pan bottom, on a cutting board. While it is still warm, cut the shortbread into quarters using a thin, sharp knife or a pizza cutter, and then cut each quarter into 4 wedges. (These will be too hard to cut if you let the shortbread cool completely.) Using a narrow metal spatula, carefully transfer the wedges to a rack to cool.

STORE in an airtight container for up to 3 weeks.

Sachertorte Bars

MAKES *32* BARS

Borrowing the components from the famous Viennese Sachertorte (pronounced *SAH-khuhr-tohrt*), which is a chocolate cake spread with apricot preserves and enrobed in dark chocolate, these bars have a fudgy brownie base and the same rich glazes. I'll bet the Austrian prince for whom pastry chef Franz Sacher created the much-celebrated cake in 1832 would have liked these just as well . . . or even better!

12	tablespoons (1½ sticks) unsalted butter
5	ounces unsweetened chocolate, coarsely chopped
2	cups sugar
4	large eggs
2	teaspoons pure vanilla extract
½	teaspoon salt
1⅓	cups all-purpose flour
½	cup apricot preserves

CHOCOLATE GANACHE GLAZE

4	ounces good-quality bittersweet chocolate, chopped
½	cup heavy cream
2	teaspoons light corn syrup

PREHEAT the oven to 350°F. Line a 9 × 13-inch baking pan with foil that extends about 2 inches over each of the short sides. Butter the foil.

MELT the butter and chocolate in a large saucepan over very low heat, stirring often, until melted and smooth. Remove the pan from the heat and whisk in the sugar. Whisk in the eggs, one at a time. Mix in the vanilla and salt. Using a rubber spatula, stir in the flour until fully incorporated. Spread the batter in the prepared pan and smooth the top with the spatula. Bake for 23 to 25 minutes or until the top is just firm to the touch. Cool on a rack to room temperature.

COMBINE the apricot preserves and 1 teaspoon of water in a small saucepan. Heat, stirring and mashing any chunks of fruit with a fork, over low heat for 1 minute.

HOLDING on to the foil overhang, lift the brownie out of the pan and place it on a rack. Peel away the foil from the sides of the brownie. Place a cutting board over the brownie and carefully invert the brownie onto the board. Remove the rack and gently peel off the foil.

BRUSH the warm apricot preserves over the top of the brownie (which was the bottom). Discard any chunks of apricot. Let stand for 10 minutes.

FOR THE CHOCOLATE GANACHE GLAZE: Place the chocolate in a heat-proof bowl. Bring the cream and corn syrup to a simmer in a small saucepan. Carefully pour the cream mixture over the chocolate. Whisk gently until the chocolate melts and the mixture is smooth. Refrigerate the glaze for about 15 minutes or let stand at room temperature until it's thickened slightly but still pourable. Pour the chocolate over the apricot glaze, spreading it evenly with an offset spatula or small rubber spatula. Let stand at room temperature for 2 to 3 hours or until the chocolate glaze is set.

USING a thin-bladed knife (and wiping off the blade after each slice), cut the brownie into quarters lengthwise, then cut crosswise into 8 strips for a total of 32 bars.

STORE, layered between sheets of wax paper, in an airtight container for up to 2 days; or refrigerate for up to 5 days. If chilled, let sit at room temperature for at least 30 minutes to soften before serving. The (unglazed) brownie cake, wrapped securely in plastic wrap, can be kept at room temperature for up to 3 days or frozen for up to 2 months.

Lemon Squares

Everyone seems to have their own idea of what makes the perfect lemon square. Some prefer more (or less) crust, some demand a double lemon layer that's mouth-puckeringly tart, and others insist that the crust and lemon topping be exactly the same thickness. I side with the fifty-fifty crowd, but I wanted to bake my luscious lemony topping over a brown-sugar shortbread crust. I hope you'll find that these squares satisfy every lemon lover.

CRUST

1¾   cups all-purpose flour
⅓   cup packed light brown sugar
¼   teaspoon salt
12   tablespoons (1½ sticks) chilled unsalted butter, cut into small chunks

TOPPING

5   large eggs
2¼   cups granulated sugar
1   tablespoon finely grated lemon zest
¾   cup fresh lemon juice (from about 4 lemons)
⅓   cup all-purpose flour
   Confectioners' sugar, for dusting

FOR THE CRUST: Preheat the oven to 350°F. Have ready an ungreased 9 × 13-inch baking pan.

PLACE the flour, brown sugar, and salt in a food processor. Pulse a few times to combine, making sure there are no lumps of sugar remaining. Add the butter and process until the dough becomes crumbly; it will look dry, but it should feel moist when pinched. Spread the dough in the pan, pressing down to form a smooth, even layer. Bake for 20 to 22 minutes or until the crust is golden brown. Transfer the pan to a rack and let the crust cool to room temperature, about 20 minutes. Reduce the oven temperature to 300°F.

FOR THE TOPPING: Whisk the eggs in a large bowl. Add the sugar and whisk until smooth. Whisk in the lemon zest, lemon juice, and flour. Pour the lemon mixture over the cooled crust. Bake for 30 to 35 minutes or until the topping is set and doesn't wiggle when the pan is moved. Transfer the pan to a rack to cool completely.

USING a thin, sharp knife or a bench scraper, cut lengthwise into quarters, then cut crosswise into 6 strips for a total of 24 squares. Carefully remove the squares from the pan using a thin metal spatula. Just before serving, dust the lemon squares with confectioners' sugar.

STORE, layered between sheets of wax paper, in an airtight container in the refrigerator for up to 5 days.

Toffee Bars

MAKES *32* TO *48* BARS (DEPENDING ON HOW THEY'RE CUT)

These candy-like cookies are rich and satisfying; just a few bites go a long way. Use a fine-quality bittersweet chocolate, not semisweet chocolate chips, for the best results.

1	cup natural (unblanched) almonds, chopped
16	tablespoons (2 sticks) unsalted butter
1	cup packed light brown sugar
1½	teaspoons pure vanilla extract
½	teaspoon salt
2	cups all-purpose flour
10	ounces fine-quality bittersweet chocolate, chopped

PREHEAT the oven to 350°F. Line a 10½ × 15½ × 1-inch jelly roll pan with foil, pressing the foil into the corners and leaving about 2 inches hanging over both short sides. Generously butter or grease the foil.

PLACE the almonds on a small baking sheet and toast in the oven, stirring a few times, for 6 to 8 minutes or until golden. (Watch carefully that the smaller bits don't get too brown.)

MELT the butter in a medium saucepan over low heat. Remove the pan from the heat and stir in the brown sugar, making sure there are no lumps remaining. Stir in the vanilla and salt. Add the flour and mix well until thoroughly blended.

TRANSFER the dough to the prepared pan. Using your fingers or a rubber spatula, spread the dough evenly. (You might think there won't be enough, but persevere . . . it fits!) Bake in the middle of the oven for 18 to 20 minutes or until the crust is nicely browned all over. (If your jelly roll pan is insulated as many are, it will probably take the longer time.) Cool on a rack for 5 minutes.

WHILE the crust bakes, melt the chocolate in a medium stainless-steel or glass bowl set over a saucepan of barely simmering water, stirring frequently, until fully melted. Transfer the bowl of chocolate to a rack to cool for a few minutes.

POUR the chocolate over the crust and use a rubber spatula to spread it evenly. Sprinkle with the toasted almonds. Cool in the pan on a rack until the chocolate is set, about 2 hours. (You can speed up the cooling by placing the pan in the refrigerator, if desired.)

HOLDING on to the foil overhang, carefully lift up the bars and place them on a cutting board. Peel the foil away from the sides of the bars. Using a bench scraper or a sharp knife, cut into quarters lengthwise. Turn the pan so it's horizontally in front of you and cut crosswise into quarters; then cut each quarter section into 2 or 3 strips. Eight strips across the pan will yield 32 bars; 12 strips across will yield 48 bars.

STORE, layered between sheets of wax paper, in an airtight container for up to 1 week; or refrigerate for up to 2 weeks; or freeze for up to 3 months.

Turtle Bars

MAKES *24* TO *48* BARS (DEPENDING ON HOW THEY'RE CUT)

If you know turtles—not the slow-moving kind, but the chocolate-covered caramel candies with pecans jutting out to look like a turtle's head and feet—then you've tasted how dreamy that trio of flavors is. Now add a buttery brown sugar crust and you've got what's known as turtle bars, which I guarantee will be swiftly gobbled up by cookie lovers of all ages.

CRUST

12	tablespoons (1½ sticks) unsalted butter
½	cup packed light brown sugar
¼	teaspoon salt
2	cups all-purpose flour

CARAMEL TOPPING

1⅓	cups granulated sugar
1	cup heavy cream
5	tablespoons unsalted butter, cut into 5 slices
1	teaspoon pure vanilla extract
½	teaspoon salt
2	cups pecans, toasted, cooled, and coarsely chopped

CHOCOLATE DRIZZLE

4	ounces bittersweet chocolate, chopped

FOR THE CRUST: Preheat the oven to 350°F. Lightly grease a 9 × 13-inch baking pan. Line the pan with a sheet of foil, leaving a 2-inch overhang at both short sides. Butter or grease the foil, covering the bottom and sides fully. (The reason for greasing the pan before lining it with foil is to help the foil adhere so it doesn't move around when you press in the crust.)

MELT the butter in a medium saucepan over low heat. Remove from the heat and stir in the brown sugar and salt, breaking up any lumps of sugar. Add the flour and mix until thoroughly blended. Using your fingers, spread the dough evenly in the prepared pan. (Yes, it fits!) Bake for about 18 minutes or until golden brown. Transfer the pan to a rack to cool while you make the caramel. (Maintain the oven temperature.)

FOR THE CARAMEL TOPPING: Place the granulated sugar in a large, heavy saucepan and set over moderately low heat. Cook, undisturbed, until the sugar begins to melt around the edge. Continue to cook, stirring occasionally with a wooden spoon, until the sugar is almost fully melted, then stir constantly to melt the remaining bits. The melted sugar should be a deep golden caramel color. (Melting the sugar will take about 6 to 9 minutes.)

CAREFULLY pour in the cream. The caramel will bubble wildly and immediately harden. Lower the heat slightly and simmer, stirring constantly, until the hardened caramel melts, about 7 to 10 minutes. Remove the pan from the heat and stir in the butter, vanilla, and salt. When the butter is fully melted, stir in the pecans. Immediately pour the caramel over the crust, spreading it to the edges. Return the pan to the oven and bake for about 18 minutes. The caramel will be bubbling and still a little liquidy; it will set as it cools. Transfer to a rack to cool completely, about 2 hours.

HOLDING on to the foil overhang, carefully lift the bars from the pan and place on a cutting board. Peel away the foil from the sides of the bars, using a bench scraper or a thin knife to assist, if needed.

FOR THE CHOCOLATE DRIZZLE: Melt the chocolate in a microwave-safe bowl in the microwave for 20- to 30-second intervals on medium power, stirring after each interval, until melted and smooth. Dip a fork or a small spoon in the chocolate and drizzle the chocolate over the bars. Let the chocolate set before cutting.

USING a sharp knife or a bench scraper, cut into quarters lengthwise, then cut crosswise into 6 strips for a total of 24 bars. Since these are so rich, the bars are best cut in half again for a total of 48 bars. Alternatively, cut into 8 strips crosswise for a total of 32 bars.

STORE, layered between sheets of wax paper, in an airtight container for up to 1 week; or refrigerate for up to 2 weeks; or freeze for up to 3 months.

No-Bake Treats

Tips FOR MAKING NO-BAKE TREATS

Sometimes a great treat requires no oven. The mixture relies instead on melted chocolate, marshmallow, peanut butter, or a little liquid to bind a few delectable ingredients.

- For no-bake treats, it's especially important to remember my opening words about using fresh, quality ingredients, because whatever you toss into the mixing bowl is what you'll taste.

Use good-quality chocolate and peanut butter, tender marshmallows, fresh nuts, and graham crackers and wafers that aren't soggy or stale.

- Once you've combined all the ingredients, don't let the mixture sit too long before either transferring it to a pan or shaping it. It will end up hardening in the bowl.

Chocolate Hearts (page 128)

Rocky Road Bites

MAKES *32* BARS

For those of you whose favorite ice-cream flavor is Rocky Road, the same heavenly combination—chocolate, marshmallows, and walnuts—comes together in these bite-size cookie-candies. The only hard part about this recipe is waiting for the chocolate to set!

10	ounces fine-quality bittersweet or semisweet chocolate, chopped
2	tablespoons unsalted butter
1 ½	cups mini marshmallows
1 ¼	cups walnuts, toasted and coarsely chopped
6	graham cracker squares (3 full rectangles), broken into ½-inch pieces (about 1 full cup) (see Note)

LINE an 8-inch square pan with foil, pressing the foil into the corners and leaving a 2-inch overhang on two opposite sides.

MELT the chocolate and butter in a large metal or glass bowl set over a saucepan of barely simmering water; stir constantly. When the chocolate is almost fully melted, remove the bowl from the heat and stir to melt the remaining pieces. Let cool at room temperature for 5 minutes.

STIR in 1 cup of the marshmallows, 1 cup of the walnuts, and all the graham cracker pieces. Spread the mixture in the prepared pan. Sprinkle evenly with the remaining ½ cup of marshmallows and ¼ cup of walnuts, pressing down lightly so they adhere. Let stand at room temperature until the chocolate sets, about 2 hours; or refrigerate for about 1 hour.

HOLDING on to the foil overhang, lift up the bars and place on a cutting board. Peel away the foil from the sides of the bars. Using a bench scraper or a sharp knife, cut into 16 squares, then cut each square in half to make 32 small bars.

STORE, layered between sheets of wax paper, in an airtight container for up to 1 week; or refrigerate for up to 3 weeks.

NOTE: If you don't have graham crackers, any plain, crisp cookie will do.

Peanut Butter Chocolate Squares

MAKES *32* SQUARES

If you're a peanut butter lover or know some hungry children who are, try these easy, no-bake treats. They are the perfect snack, along with a mug of hot cocoa, after a day of skiing, skating, or snowshoeing. And if your peanut passion knows no bounds, sprinkle about ½ cup finely chopped salted peanuts over the chocolate just after spreading it.

26 graham cracker squares (13 full rectangles)

16 tablespoons (2 sticks) unsalted butter

1 cup creamy peanut butter

2½ cups confectioners' sugar

12 ounces semisweet chocolate, chopped (or substitute semisweet chocolate chips)

HAVE ready an ungreased 9 × 13-inch baking pan.

BREAK up the graham crackers and place them in a food processor. Process into crumbs. (Alternatively, place the crackers in a sturdy plastic bag and crush them with the smooth side of a meat mallet.) You should have about 2 cups of crumbs.

MELT the butter in a large saucepan over low heat. Remove from the heat and stir in the peanut butter, mixing well until smooth. Stir in the confectioners' sugar and graham cracker crumbs. Scrape the mixture into the baking pan and, using your fingers or a rubber spatula, press down evenly to form a smooth layer.

MELT the chocolate in a large metal or glass bowl set over a saucepan of barely simmering water; stir constantly. When melted, pour the chocolate over the peanut butter base and spread it evenly with a rubber spatula.

REFRIGERATE the pan for about 30 minutes or let stand at room temperature until the chocolate is almost set. (If you wait to cut the squares until the chocolate is completely set, the chocolate will be difficult to cut.) Using a bench scraper or a thin-bladed knife, cut into quarters lengthwise, then cut crosswise into 8 strips for a total of 32 squares.

STORE, layered between sheets of wax paper, in an airtight container for up to 5 days; or refrigerate for up to 3 weeks; or freeze for up to 3 months.

Chocolate Hearts

MAKES ABOUT *22* COOKIES

This recipe comes from Corinne Planche, who took the beautiful photographs in this book. Corinne grew up in Geneva, Switzerland, and these chocolate hearts were Christmas favorites. Read through the recipe and you'll see how unusual this cookie is: No flour. No butter. No eggs. No baking! The dough is assembled from ground almonds, chocolate, sugar, and a few spoonfuls of kirsch (pronounced *keersh*), a cherry brandy, and then it's rolled out, stamped into hearts, and left to dry overnight. Corinne tells me that all Swiss cooks keep kirsch (also called *Kirschwasser*, which in German means "cherry water") in the house because it's a necessary ingredient for fondue.

5 ounces good-quality bittersweet chocolate, chopped

2 cups (about 8 ounces) finely ground blanched almonds or almond meal (see Note)

¾ cup sugar, plus more for rolling out the dough

3 tablespoons kirsch

NOTE: Almond meal or flour, which is finely ground blanched almonds, is sold in some specialty markets. It's also available online from bobsredmill.com and kingarthurflour.com.

COOKIE CUTTER NEEDED: heart measuring about 2½ inches across the top

PLACE the chocolate in a food processor and process until finely ground. Add the ground almonds and ¾ cup of sugar and pulse a few times to combine. Add the kirsch and 2 tablespoons of water and pulse until the dough starts to hold together. If it's too crumbly, add up to 1 tablespoon more water. When you squeeze the dough it should stick together.

SPRINKLE a clean work surface with sugar. Working with half the dough at a time, place it on the sugar and roll it out to about a ⅓-inch thickness. (Sprinkle the dough with a little sugar if the rolling pin sticks to it.) Using the cookie cutter, stamp out hearts. Transfer them, using a thin metal spatula, to a rack. Reroll the scraps with the remaining dough. Let the cookies dry on the rack overnight to firm up.

STORE, layered between sheets of wax paper, in an airtight container for up to 2 weeks; or freeze for up to 3 months.

Rum Balls

MAKES ABOUT *42* BALLS

I remember my mother making something like these—she says she used pound-cake crumbs instead of wafers—and giving me a taste when I was a child. Frankly, I wondered how anything that looked so rich and chocolaty could taste so bad! The rum flavor was pretty potent! As my tastes matured, however, these grown-up treats, which resemble chocolate rum truffles, have become welcome at our holiday celebrations.

Rolling the dough into balls is messy, sticky fun. You can also use a mini–ice cream scoop—size #100 (measuring 2 teaspoons) is perfect for the job—to form rounded scoopfuls of dough. Drop the balls into either cocoa powder or confectioners' sugar, or try some of each. They're a tad less sweet rolled in cocoa.

2½ cups chocolate wafer crumbs (crushed from about 9 ounces chocolate wafers, such as Nabisco's Famous Chocolate Wafers)
1 cup finely chopped walnuts
1 cup confectioners' sugar
2 tablespoons unsweetened cocoa powder
⅓ cup light rum
3 tablespoons light corn syrup
Additional cocoa powder and/or confectioners' sugar, for coating the rum balls

COMBINE the chocolate wafer crumbs, walnuts, confectioners' sugar, and cocoa powder in a large bowl. Add the rum and corn syrup, stirring until the mixture comes together and is thick and pasty.

PLACE about ⅓ cup of cocoa or confectioners' sugar in a small bowl. (Or use some of each in two separate bowls.) Roll the dough into 1-inch balls (or use a mini–ice cream scoop) and toss a few at a time in the cocoa or confectioners' sugar to coat.

STORE, layered between sheets of wax paper, in an airtight container in the refrigerator or a cool, dark place for up to 1 month (these get better with age); or freeze for up to 3 months. Serve at room temperature for the best flavor.

Recipes by Flavor

When you know you're in the mood for . . .

Cornmeal Currant Cookies 43
Cranberry Pistachio Biscotti 74
Cranberry Swirl Cheesecake Squares 110
Fig Half-Moons 101
Linzer Cookies 99

Caramel/Toffee
Chocolate Caramel Thumbprints 97
Toffee Bars 120
Turtle Bars 122

Rum
Eggnog Cookies 61
Rum Balls 129

A Few More Lists

Cookies Without Nuts
Baby Butter and Jam Sandwiches 92
Chocolate Caramel Thumbprints 97
Chocolate Crinkles 78
Chocolate Espresso Wafers 65
Chocolate Peppermint Cookies 80
Chocolate Shortbread Wedges 115
Cocoa Meringue Kisses 38
Coconut Macaroons 36
Cornmeal Currant Cookies 43
Cranberry Swirl Cheesecake Squares 110
Eggnog Cookies 61
Fig Half-Moons 101
Ginger Coins 59
Gingerbread People 55
Iced Lemon Rounds 35
Italian Wine Cookies 88
Lemon Squares 118
Molasses Ginger Cookies 77
Orange Poppy Seed Drops 76
Pinwheel Cookies 63
Sachertorte Bars 116

Sugar Cookies 46
Sugar Cookies with Stained Glass 49
Toasted Coconut Sablés 68

Quick and Easy
Cookie dough you can assemble and
    bake within one hour.

Almond Macaroons 32
Brown Sugar Pecan Cookies 30
Coconut Macaroons 36
Italian Wine Cookies 88
Lace Cookies 31
Maple Walnut Cookies 28
Mexican Chocolate Snowballs 40
Molasses Ginger Cookies 77
Orange Poppy Seed Drops 76
Peanut Brittle Bars 113
Peanut Butter Chocolate Kisses 87

Make-Ahead and Freeze Cookie Dough
These doughs can be made ahead and frozen for up to
three months.

Baby Butter and Jam Sandwiches 92
Brown Sugar Pecan Cookies 30
Chocolate Caramel Thumbprints 97
Chocolate Espresso Wafers 65
Dutch Spice Cookies 44
Eggnog Cookies 61
Fig Half-Moons 101
Ginger Coins 59
Gingerbread People 55
Lace Cookies 31
Linzer Cookies 99
Pecan Sandies 67
Pinwheel Cookies 63
Sugar Cookies 46
Toasted Coconut Sablés 68
Viennese Crescents 85

Index

MOUNT PLEASANT